First things first

The struggle between management and unions is becoming more bitter. Crime and violence are on the increase; law and order are breaking down. Family life is under pressure as parents split up and children rebel. And in an allegedly secular age, superstition is rife.

In this hard-hitting book, the author maintains that the problems of modern society can be solved only by a return to Christian principles. Based on the Ten Commandments, the book is practical, helpful and down to earth. It is also vividly illustrated from the author's own experience. The table-talk of politicians is quoted alongside the hopes and fears of housewives, students and working men.

Sir Frederick Catherwood has been Director-General of the National Economic Development Council, Chairman of the British Overseas Trade Board, Chairman of the British Institute of Management, and Chief Executive of several large companies. He is a member of the Central Religious Advisory Committee of the BBC and IBA. He is currently Chairman of Mallinson-Denny Ltd., and European MP for Cambridgeshire.

To Bethan Jane

An Aslan Lion Book

First things first

The practice of principles in modern society

Fred Catherwood

LION PUBLISHING

Copyright © Sir Frederick Catherwood 1979

LION PUBLISHING
Icknield Way, Tring, Herts

First edition 1979

ISBN 0 85648 178 5

This book is based on a series of articles originally
published in *The Evangelical Times*

Text set by Art Photoset Ltd., Beaconsfield, Bucks
and printed in Britain by Anchor Press Ltd., Colchester, Essex

Contents

Introduction

Most of us have the uneasy feeling that, despite a great many improvements, a lot of things are going badly wrong with our society. We comfort ourselves with the conviction that matters were probably much worse a hundred years ago, and that no generation believes that things are what they used to be. It is true that we are richer than we were a generation ago. In Britain, our real, spendable income has doubled since 1950. Our health is better and we live longer. We have more education – three times as many university students and four times as many professors. Our social security system makes sure that nobody starves. We have better houses, and more of them. So, if all that we have been told were true, we should have less social conflict and less crime, because the 'economic causes' of crime and conflict have been removed. But that is not what we find.

Is society improving?

Despite the doubling of our standard of living, days lost through industrial disputes have risen from 1,389,000 in 1950 to 9,985,000 in 1977, an increase of 619 per cent. The value of money has gone down over the same period by 80 per cent – the worst inflation in the history of the country, and almost entirely self-inflicted. As a direct consequence, the number of unemployed has increased by 365 per cent, from 306,000 in 1950 to 1,423,000 in 1977, with the brunt falling on young people leaving school.

If the increase of drunkenness is any indication of the national mood, we are much less happy. Convictions for drunkenness have risen by 130 per cent from 55,800 in 1950 to

128,400 in 1977. Nobody who marries wants their new partnership to end in divorce, for divorce is a traumatic event, leaving scars on the couple and unhappiness for the children. But divorces have increased by 393 per cent from 29,096 in 1950 to 128,400 in 1976.

Broken marriages are one of the main causes of juvenile crime. Crimes of violence against the person committed by juveniles in England and Wales have risen by an astounding 1,582 per cent, from 315 to 5,300 in the same period. This is only part of the crimewave. All offences have increased by 182 per cent, crimes of violence against the person in England and Wales have risen by 900 per cent from 3,839 to 38,400, and the number of murders in the whole country has risen by 478 per cent from 38 to 220.

These are some of the figures of the so-called 'permissive society'. We have decided, in the last generation, that society has come of age, and no longer needs the old restraints of law and custom. We are sophisticated and knowledgeable, and can do without such restrictions. We no longer need to go to church. The numbers on the electoral roll of the Church of England have dropped by nearly one third from 2.9 million in 1950 to 2 million in 1976. The number of Easter communicants was down to 1.7 million, and the number at ordinary Sunday services down to 1.2 million. Other Christian churches suffered the same kind of fall, with the exception of the newly-arrived Afro-West Indian churches and the Pentecostals. Even those who went to church were not sure whether they would hear the traditional Christian message. From 'honest to God' to 'the myth of God incarnate', the liberal wing of the church seemed to go along with the national mood.

If there is one certain prediction, it is that these permissive trends cannot go on without affecting the structure of British society. Violence breeds violence. If people cannot get protection from the law, they tend to take the law into their own hands. Already those who can afford it pay for private protection. Companies keep armies of private guards, and the rich do not let their children go far without a private detective. But the poor, the old and the weak have to suffer from violence, and the fear and isolation which it brings.

Confrontation
In industrial relations, a few mavericks can hold their fellow-

workers to ransom for more money. The aims of the trades union movement are being stood on their head. The bargaining power of the few is being used for themselves, and not to help weaker comrades in the union. As company profits are squeezed, the investment on which higher earnings and new jobs depend is discouraged, and the rate of unemployment rises. Incomes policies are cobbled together, survive a year or so, and then break up. Confrontation is tried and then compromise attempted, but neither seems to succeed.

A great many people put their faith in politics for the answers. But politicians have to deal with society as it is. A good politician will bring out the best in us, and a poor one may bring out the worst. But few politicians can stand against the strong tides of public opinion. They have to act within the limitations of what the majority of people will accept. They cannot impose morality by law, if the law will not be respected. Such attempts to impose standards have been catastrophic failures in Britain and elsewhere.

The real battle is not fought between government and opposition in Parliament; it is the stuggle for people's minds and hearts and takes place in everyday conversation. We cannot blame the politicians. They do the best they can, but are bound to reflect the society in which they live.

We should not ask our political leaders to set up moral standards. When Prime Minister Harold Macmillan was asked to give a moral judgement he said, 'That is a matter for the bishops.' For politicians too must be judged by moral standards, and we must not leave them free to set up their own. That is totalitarianism. We need a standard of reference to which we can take the issues of our day, and by which we can judge them. In Britain, for a thousand years, that standard has been the Christian faith. Our generation has decided that they can dispense with it; but the swift deterioration in our society entitles us to suggest that they are wrong.

Is Britain Christian?

It is often argued that, since Britain is no longer a Christian country, we are not entitled to make the Christian faith our standard of reference. But immigrants of other religions constitute only a tiny minority in the country. In the survey of church membership in 1975, there were 111,000 Jews, 21,000 Buddhists, 100,000 Hindus, 400,000 Muslims and 115,000

Sikhs – a total of no more than three-quarters of a million, against a total of nearly eight million in the much-reduced Christian churches. Nor is it the immigrant groups or the Jews who demand the dismantling of the standards which have served for so long the country to which they come. Their own moral codes are much tougher and tighter than the one they find around them. They battle against the permissive society even more fiercely than the Christians. They are amazed that we let go our standards, that we no longer respect our age-old faith. And the biggest immigrant group of all is served by the Afro-West Indian churches who do not integrate because they distrust the declining standards of the British churches.

So, in the absence of an agreed moral basis, we are in danger of finding that might is right. Even politicians talk of keeping industrial peace by 'giving the lions the lions' share'.

The intellectuals, who for the last generation have led society into the present morass, argue that in a scientific age man can no longer be governed by the superstitions of religion. They are helped in this view by churchmen who are not prepared to challenge the right of such people to claim scientific support for speculations which cannot be measured or proved by the scientific method.

I once sat on a government committee with one of our greatest scientists, at that time President of the Royal Society. Britain would have starved in World War II without his inventiveness. One day over lunch we talked about 'accidental evolution'. I told him that I found the whole idea quite incredible; that everywhere in the natural world there was design: in the cycle of food production, in the balance of nature, and in the human eye with its self-adjusting light aperture, its self-adjusting focus, its automatic blink and tear-ducts and its colour sensitivity. I said, 'How can all this design possibly be the result of accident? Design like that must have a designer.' 'On the evidence we have,' he replied, 'you are just as entitled to believe in design as I am to believe in evolution by accident. I can only say that it's amazing what can happen over millions and millions of years.'

But human lives are not given millions and millions of years. Only three or four years later, a few months before his death, I saw the same man in the library of our club, a gaunt, gloomy, silent figure, hunched over the fire, staring into nothing, face to face with oblivion. When I left the club some time later, he was standing in the rain without a coat. I offered him a lift; he told me not to bother. He had come to the end, and nothing seemed to matter any more.

According to his beliefs, death was as natural as the falling of an autumn leaf. But when it looked him in the face, he looked back at it with blank despair. If we are no more than an accident, why do we regard death as a tragedy? Christianity teaches that this is because it *is* a tragedy. Man was made to live, and not to die. We have a feeling inside that there is something wrong about death, something evil – and so there is. Our horror of death is a justified horror.

Any view of mankind, religious or irreligious, has to deal with the apparent contradictions of life and death, good and evil. You cannot deal with one without the other. Fashionable intellectual opinion of our day tends to ignore death, and treats evil as though it were a curable disease. So death is a taboo subject – as sex was for the Victorians. We know it happens, but it is not mentioned in polite circles as happening to us. It makes us feel awkward and embarrassed. We do not know how to talk about it.

But violence, and all the other growing evils of our society, cannot be so easily swept under the carpet. When the retired chief of Britain's largest police force says that his former force can no longer defend the property of the citizen, we know that the truth is out. When responsible people begin refusing to identify those who have attacked them, because they fear retaliation, we know it is no longer merely the citizen's property which the police are unable to protect. Just as the pilferage which adds three per cent to the supermarket prices is not carried out by starving people, so attacks on people are not made for money, but 'because they enjoy it'.

Christian guidelines
It is time we recognized the permissive society for the danger-ous fiasco that it is. We must get back to the guide-lines which have lifted our society from pagan superstition and violence. Over the centuries they tamed the rapacity of rulers, brought us out of servitude and serfdom, established the rule of law, encouraged education, science, economic development and free institutions, and promoted freedom of speech and equality of opportunity. Instead of despising all that has ever gone before, we need to consider the mainsprings which made our

society what it was, and especially the standards of conduct accepted as the ultimate point of reference.

No Christian pretends that society was perfect until a generation ago. It is not part of Christian teaching that moral precepts will make a man a Christian, nor that a nation's people are Christian, merely because it has a Christian church established by law. But Christianity teaches that a dedicated Christian community can gain the respect of those who are not themselves committed Christians. Society's respect for Christian standards will make it a healthier and happier society.

No Christian pretends that he can keep to Christian standards all of the time. All of us slip; nobody is is perfect. Only the Pharisee considers himself beyond reproach. The apostle Paul considered himself 'the chief of sinners'. Christians and their families are affected by society and it is a continual struggle to keep to the standards of the faith. The struggle is made no easier by society's insistence on removing so many of the customs which once protected us all, but especially the young, from rash moments of unconsidered folly.

But the Christian who sets these standards for himself is sorry when he fails – and when those about him fail. And the Christian has a duty to pass on to others the standards by which all humanity will one day be judged. These are our Maker's instructions about our duty to him and to each other. This book looks again at those instructions – the Ten Commandments.

Chapter 1

Restoring the foundations

I am the Lord your God . . . You shall have no other gods before me.
You shall love the Lord your God with all your heart, and with all your soul, and with all your mind.

We live today in what is carelessly called a secular society. That means, putting it bluntly, that people do not care about God any more. They do not care whether he exists or not. It just does not matter. They have put it out of their minds. It is a vast irrelevance.

If you press them, people think science has somehow proved that there is no God and dispensed with the need for him. Science is the bountiful provider. If there are temporary shortages – for instance of energy, or food for the Third World – science will think up the answers in the future, as it has in the past.

Yet there is the beginning of an uneasy feeling that maybe this touching faith in science is too blind. We are becoming frightened of science, frightened that its power will get out of control. And not only are we frightened of science; superstitious fear has also crept out of the cracks and crevices, and science cannot keep it back.

But the Christian faith teaches that God is at the centre of life. Whether we believe in him or not, he is still there. What does our opinion do to change God? We are here today and gone tomorrow. He always was and always will be. It is nothing but blind arrogance for the creature to sit in judgement on the Creator.

A cheerful American girl called Becky told me that for a long time she couldn't bring herself to believe in God. It was all too fantastic, too unreal. Then one day she was lying on the grass outside her home, and noticed the ants hurrying to and fro. She thought, 'I wonder if those ants believe in Becky?' She guessed they probably did not. To them she was a hill, a large shadow. How could they possibly believe in her – she was too different, too complex, too unlike anything they could know about or imagine. She picked up some of the ants and let them run about in her hand. 'Even now', she thought, 'they don't believe in me. I'm just a surface area. They don't realize I'm looking at them, that I could clap my hands together and kill them.'

Then it suddenly dawned on Becky that God might be to her just as she was to the ants. No matter how much she dismissed him, he might still be there, watching her, powerful but waiting. It was that thought which shook her out of her arrogance and made her reflect. It led her to people who could teach her, and bring her to a knowledge of God as Creator and Saviour.

Unlike Becky's ants, we can hear God. He has spoken to the men and women he created. He spoke through prophets and through conscience. He also revealed himself systematically, clearly and logically through the Jewish law, and then face-to-face in Jesus Christ, who was both God and man.

Christ was asked what he considered the greatest commandment. He answered, 'The Lord our God, the Lord is one; and you shall love the Lord your God with all your heart, and with all your soul, and with all your mind, and with all your strength.' He then added, 'The second is this, "You shall love your neighbour as yourself."'

Many people today agree with the second commandment which we call 'the golden rule'. But the second command depends on the first. Society today breaks the second command on a grand scale because it has broken the first. The second command has no authority without the first. People want to know why they should love their neighbour.

I once appeared on a television programme with an archbishop, who had just made a public appeal for financial restraint, and a trades union leader whom I knew well. Before we went on the air, the union leader asked me: 'What's he on about, Fred? Why shouldn't my members want a bit more money? What's wrong with a bit more money?' When the programme started, I suggested to the archbishop that it was not enough to tell people what to do. Everybody from politicians to newspaper editors does that. With his authority as head of the nation's largest church he had to explain *why*.

The original first commandment, as recorded in Exodus 20:

2–3 is: 'I am the Lord your God, who brought you out of the land of Egypt, out of the house of bondage. You shall have no other gods before me.' When the commandment is repeated in Deuteronomy we read 'The Lord our God is one Lord.' 'You shall fear the Lord your God; you shall serve him.'

The need for authority

These passages give us a picture of the character of God, especially of his authority. Ours is a permissive age and we do not like authority. We do not like to contemplate a being who has the right to tell us what to do and what not to do. It is not really our knowledge of science which turns us against God – science has no standing in the issue – but our dislike of authority. We cherish our freedom, even if it is illusory. We want to reserve to ourselves the right to judge right and wrong. We persuade ourselves that wise men can agree and that there is no need for any external authority.

We are beginning to find out that this is false. I have worked for over a dozen years at the conference tables where men try to get agreement: as industrial adviser to the government, at the National Economic Development Council, at the British Institute of Management, and at the Overseas Trade Board. In all these debates we come down in the end to the question of authority. The owners believe that authority depends on ownership, the government believes it depends on democratic election, trades unions believe it belongs to organized labour, the shop-floor believes that it belongs to them.

Disagreement about authority is disastrous. Who is to persuade the coal-miners that they should not go-slow or strike? Who is to persuade other unions that they should not aim for the pay-award given to the miners? What if the middle-classes, in exasperation, stop paying their taxes? A prime minister once slipped me a message at a meeting. It read: 'What is the matter with everyone? Why can't they be content with a fair day's work for a fair day's pay? Do me a note on it.' Well might he ask!

We have never been more affluent, never had more social security, more education, more health care, or longer expectation of life. But not for a long time have we had so much violence in society. In the first twenty-five years of the Queen's reign, murder almost quadrupled, and juvenile crimes of violence against the person multiplied seventeen times. Words fail me to describe this outbreak of violence by the young, strong and well-fed against the old and weak. What authority is going to instil sweet reason into them – or into the mob-violence of football fanatics? There is no such authority in sight. Secular society has no answer. It is already a disastrous failure. If every man does what is right in his own eyes, the end result is chaos.

No doubt many people believe that all we need is strong government. The call for firmer government is going to get louder. But without a moral code which is higher and stronger than the strongest government, what check is there on government?

Democracy has only survived for any length of time in countries which have held to a Christian moral code – and not in all of those. Nobody knows whether democracy can survive in a secular society. I doubt it. Strong governments, called to power in societies which have thrown over their moral code, tend to make up rules for their own convenience as they go along. As the Watergate scandal in the USA has shown us, even governments in democracies justify to themselves all kinds of illegal action for so-called 'reasons of state'. The totalitarian state imposes its own morality to support itself in power. It hounds the non-conformist to death. Strong government is not the answer to violence.

Mankind needs an external authority. It needs a final point of reference on which law and custom can be based, and a common belief, held widely through society, by which arguments can finally be settled. Christianity has provided that reference point. For hundreds of years it has checked the arrogance of principalities and powers. It has reformed the church itself, and edged back selfishness and greed. It has not made a perfect society, for there is no such thing in this world. But it built a society capable of reform, capable of putting right what was patently wrong. It has made a society with a conscience not just among a minority, but in both public opinion and among vested-interests. This is a healing factor which we have now lost. That healing factor is a belief in a God who is self-existent, independent, eternal, the foundation of all being and power. Belief in a God who is outside our little world, on whom we are utterly dependent, and whom we defy and disobey at our peril. 'The fear of God is the beginning of wisdom.' We have lost that fear and accompanying wisdom.

Science and superstition

But other fears are beginning to take its place. 'The Lord our God, the Lord is one.' Christians believe in a unity in the natural order, a unity in the universe. We believe that God made the hills and the valleys, the seas and the stars. That belief in the unity of creation is the foundation of the scientific method. The melting point of steel is the same, under the same conditions, anywhere on earth. There is unity in natural laws.

But remove the belief in one God, and we have the possibility of quite different laws 'out there'. We are back to the space-lords and time-lords of *Dr Who*. We begin to listen for sounds from outer space, and to look for unidentified flying objects. The universe becomes a potentially hostile place. The twinkling friendly star becomes a menacing space-ship, against which there is no known defence.

We read in the Bible that the God who created the universe was a God of order. He made the animals and plants according to their kinds, with the result that we can catalogue and list them. The belief in an orderly universe is another foundation of the scientific method. But the rising generation does not see order in the universe. Painting, music, and the other arts which reflect what man feels all show disorder. That is how the new pagan feels about the world around him.

Christians also believe that the universe was created by a God of reason. We find reason from beginning to end of the Bible. God tells us not only what he wants us to do, but why. God argues rationally with mankind. He teaches cause and effect in human and divine relations. Belief in a rational universe is part and parcel of the scientific method. The men who defined the scientific method believed that the Bible was the book of God's words. They felt that they should examine the book of God's works with the same reverence. They found reason in the Bible – so they would find reason in nature. And they did. They were able to build up rational systems on the basis of a uniform and orderly creation. They did not try to impose their systems on nature, as ancient philosophers had done. They learnt through the experimental method the ways in which one part of nature relates to another. So they were able to use all its powers to help mankind.

But modern man does not believe in a God of reason. If we look again at the arts – at the cinema, the theatre, at literature – we find a strong growth of the irrational. There is the feeling that there is no rhyme or reason in life. It is all absurd, a bad joke. There is no beginning, no ending, no goal; just continued, meaningless existence. The beliefs on which the scientific method was based are vanishing.

Another pillar of the scientific method is the Christian belief in an unchanging God. God's word is truth. He keeps his word, and promised Noah after the great universal catastrophe of the flood, 'While the earth remains, seedtime and harvest, cold and heat, summer and winter, day and night, shall not cease.' So we believe that God's creation is stable, not because a brief 400 years of scientific measurement have shown that there is stability, but because God, who is true, has promised stability.

This belief that there are fixed natural laws is essential to the scientific method. Experiment is worthwhile because what is true today and yesterday will remain true tommorow. The laws of science are not only uniform, orderly and rational now, but will remain so over time.

The Bible does not teach that nature has always been stable. There have been two great natural catastrophes, the flood in the time of Noah, and the harsh change in nature when Adam and Eve disobeyed God. And the Bible gives us no reason to believe that God created the world by the same natural laws with which he now sustains it. So all attempts to discover or time the origins of man and of the universe are outside the scope of the scientific method. The natural laws then and now are not the same. As the founders of the method laid down: primary causes (how the world came into being) must be separated from secondary causes (how it works now). They argued that the scientific method was about secondary causes, and that man was not competent to enquire into the primary cause.

The knowledge that we can unleash a nuclear holocaust which might set off an unstoppable fire has lent some support to the fears of natural catastrophe. And people without belief in God, have every reason to fear. It is a short step from fear to superstition. The new pagan is beginning to take that step back to the superstitions of the old paganism. I once said to a trades union leader that, with the growth of superstition, his members would soon want to consult a horoscope before they let him call a strike. He replied, 'They already do.'

In the Book of Deuteronomy God prohibits divination. He

prohibits astrologers, observing the signs of the zodiac, enchanters, witches, mediums, wizards and those who listen for voices from the dead (necromancers). All these are condemned as 'an abomination to the Lord'. And every one of them is back in Britain today. Modern man is fast drifting back to the old paganism, from which Christianity had largely liberated us for so long.

We need to hear a little less about scientific man who has no time for God. The great growth of scientific knowledge in the last three hundred years depends on a belief in God as revealed in the Bible. It grew in Christian countries. But with the denial of faith, science is giving way to superstition. The darkness and fear of the jungle is reaching back into our life.

We may think that science is by now so well established that nothing can shake it. But a professor of physical science at Cambridge told me that there is a strong reaction against science among those coming up to the university. He believes that in the past scientists have been too arrogant, claiming too much for science. They have made it an ultimate judge of everything, putting it above morality.

Today the young are suspicious of science. They distrust its claims, are disturbed by its power, and want to subject scientific developments to strict moral control. The professor believed that the physical sciences had to give up their inflated claims to play God. They must be limited to the original terms of the scientific method – a study of secondary causes. They should measure what can be measured, and not treat hypotheses based on unprovable assumptions as science.

Science has not – and cannot – prove there is no God. We can only discover him if he chooses to reveal himself. We cannot begin to keep the first commandment unless we read God's word – the Bible. There we can find out who God is, and what he says. We have to begin at the beginning. To believe in God we must know him. To do God's will, we must first find out what it is.

Discover the facts

Most people today do not even bother to take these first steps. We read the newspapers from cover to cover. We read detailed accounts of pop stars, footballers, actors, TV personalities, and, if we are more serious, of politicians and other leading figures. But we assume that we know all that needs to be known about God. Or, because there are other religions besides Christianity, we treat it like one political party among half a dozen claiming our attention. Not that we know anything about any of the rest, so that we could discover where Christianity differs from the world religions.

The very least our common sense should tell us is that we should try to discover something of the faith which has influenced our country so strongly for a thousand years. It is the faith which is common to the main industrial democracies of which we are one.

If you have not read them before, you might start by reading the four accounts of Christ's life in the New Testament, together with the Acts of the Apostles. Then go back to the Old Testament. Try starting with the historical books, the Psalms and Proverbs. Then read the shorter letters of Paul and Peter, and the Letter of James.

Regrettably, many Christians seem to be unfamiliar with the book of their faith. The wisdom of the world is pushed at us with all the power of the media, so that we have no time for the wisdom of the Creator. But the Bible explains things in a way that today's wisdom does not. It explains the odd combination of good and bad which we all find inside us. We want to do the right thing, yet often perversely do the wrong thing. We damage our relations with those we like and respect, yet seem unable somehow to help ourselves. The Bible explains, better than any psychiatrist, our resultant feeling of guilt, our urge to make amends and do better. It explains why we are so attached to life. Why we regard death as something unnatural. Why we regard it with dread and horror, as a tragedy which cannot be romanticized or prettified, but which we must all one day endure.

The Bible does not ignore the sordid side of life. It is a frank, explicit book. There is no perversion practised today which is not recorded there. But it spells out the consequences just as frankly. Sex and violence go together, moral chaos brings suffering, the morning after follows the night before.

But the Bible is not a negative book. It tells us what real love between a man and a woman should be, and can be, like. It contains one of the most beautiful love poems in literature. Its Book of Proverbs has wisdom which is true in any age. The characters it sketches are all around us: the wise and the foolish, who know it all, and will not be warned. It tells us, 'Put not your trust in princes' – a bit of advice as true today as it was then.

The Bible has had more influence than any other book in the history of mankind. It has sold more copies, and been translated into more languages and dialects than any other book.

The God of the Bible is a God of reason. He gives a reason for the first commandment. He reminds Israel that he is the Lord their God, who brought them out of bondage in Egypt. So he reminds them that he loved them, that he saved them and that he gave them freedom.

Christ gave us the same first commandment. He made it even stronger; that we should love God with all our heart, mind, soul and strength. And the reasons, too, are even stronger; that God so loved the world that he gave his only Son, that whoever believes in him should not perish but have eternal life.

God the Creator has given us all the material things we so easily take for granted: food and shelter, heat and light, family and friends, wit and beauty, love and life itself. But he has also given himself, to draw us back from our own rebellion. He wants all men, everywhere, to accept this gift.

We hear a lot today about the natural rights of men – and of women. What natural rights can anybody have who has rebelled against his Creator? What do we have that we have not been given? Our first need is to recognize our duty to God. Against him we have no rights.

One day we will have to answer our Creator face-to-face for all that we have done and said. He will require an account of the life he has given us. He will want to know how we kept the first and greatest commandment. He will want to know whether we have believed in Jesus Christ, his Son, who died so that those who believe on him might live.

Chapter 2

The gods of a secular age

You shall not make for yourselves a graven image, or any
likeness of anything that is in heaven above, or that is in
the earth beneath, or that is in the water under the earth;
you shall not bow down to them or serve them; for I the
Lord your God am a jealous God, visiting the iniquity of
the fathers upon the children to the third and fourth
generation of those who hate me, but showing steadfast
love to thousands of those who love me and keep my
commandments.

The second commandment is the longest and the most explicit
of all ten. It is the only one with a penalty and reward
attached. It is therefore a command which we neglect at our
peril. Yet we do neglect it. Because, in the countries with a
Christian culture, we do not see anybody physically bowing
down to the kind of idol worshipped by the Egyptians,
Canaanites and Syrians. That kind of idol-worship still
goes on and it is even returning to Britain with immigrants
from the Far East. But it is still alien to our culture.

The habit of erecting statues of Christian saints leads to
idolatry among the more ignorant. For the last four hundred
years statues have been strictly limited in Protestant churches.
God alone must be worshipped. We must not arrange our
church decoration so as to tempt worshippers to worship
anybody else.

God the Father is spirit. He is not confined to a body, so we
should not represent him as having a body. The relationship
between the Christian and Christ is more intimate than any
relationship between human beings. So it is misleading to
represent it by a human image. We do not worship God by
kneeling in a temple or grove before an idol. Christians
worship God in church. But we also worship him in the way we
live. We worship him by obeying his commands, by the
priorities in our life, in our songs, in the way we treat our own
bodies in which his Spirit lives. So we must not restrict the
command 'you shall not bow down to them or serve them' to
outward acts. These simply reveal inner beliefs.

When symbols become idols

It is too easy to dismiss the idols of prehistory, the idols of Africa, India, south-east Asia, and the totem poles of America, as expressing the beliefs of primitive people. But the idols were only outward symbols of a whole system of belief. They symbolize beliefs about the universe, about man's relation to nature, and relations between different groups of people; men and women, social classes, tribes and nations. The symbols were all interpreted by priests. Their view of the world was interwoven with their worship. The idol meant as much to them as football colours, a crown, a swastika, a flag or a pair of jeans do to us. On their own, they mean nothing. In context, they represent a life-style. They symbolize a common belief. Sometimes these symbols are simple, such as a football scarf. Sometimes they are very subtle, and even have a book of behaviour for the 'uninitiated' – for the life-style demands the same kind of initiation as religion.

Now of course not all customs and symbols are wrong. They are only wrong if they make up part of a system of worship which competes with our worship of God.

The crown is a symbol. Under a monarchy, it stands for obedience to the lawful authority. Under a republic, it may represent disobedience. In either instance, it can take the place of God. There are undoubtedly those who *live* for social status and recognition. There are snobs who make the social hierarchy, and all its titles, courtesies and manners, into a god for which they live.

I once attended a dinner at which a 'reforming' headmaster of Eton College was speaking. Most of the audience seemed to be Old Etonians. They were outraged at the changes he had made. As I recall it, he had, among other things, changed the 'Field Game' without consulting 'The Committee'. One old man got unsteadily to his feet, his whole body trembling with rage. He had been a member of 'The Committee' in 1909. Since that date, no important changes had been made without consultations with 'The Committee'.

It gradually dawned on me that, for the Old Etonians, this was not merely a school, it was a religion. Its rites had to be respected and preserved. The headmaster who had abandoned certain rituals was committing sacrilege. Nobody saw him out after the dinner. He left alone. Not long afterwards he resigned.

At the other end of the social scale there is the worship of the symbols of the manual worker such as the cloth cap. This goes with the hostility to the symbols of education or clerical or intellectual work. The Christian faith praises manual work. Christ was a carpenter. Peter was a fisherman, and Paul, with all his intellect, a tent-maker. But Christianity does not make a fetish of manual work. It is necessary, it is honourable; but we do not worship it.

The choice before us

So we are left with a problem which cannot be easily dismissed. Why does man worship idols which he himself creates? Of course rational man does not put it quite like that. He tries to make it look rational, rather than ridiculous. His first answer would be that we as Christians worship a God of our own creation. But that answer does not bear examination. However different other religions may be, apart from Christianity, they all have a human stamp. They all assume that a man saves himself by his own efforts. Christianity alone teaches that we are saved by faith alone. Christianity uniquely teaches of a God of love. Look at any heathen idol. It scowls fiercely. It may be impassive. But it displays no love. The heathen idol demands fear.

The loving God of Christianity is unique. He gave himself to free men and women from sin. They can escape by no other means – not by purgatory, offerings, prayer or sacrifice.

The Christian believes that God is Creator, holy, just and all-powerful. He also believes that God loved us enough to die for us. The Christian God is not like the gods that man invents for himself.

The Christian faith is monotheistic. It gives no other options. People do not like to be tied down to one god. We like to keep our options open. It is natural to want to be the judge. We want to be able to decide which god to choose. So we prefer to have a whole range of idols. If we do not like one, we can choose another. But we must choose, and we must have liberty of choice.

The Christian faith teaches that this was man's original sin. What did the serpent say to Eve? He questioned whether she had to obey God. He questioned her belief in what God said. A choice was open to her. She could eat the fruit and not die. From that time on her eyes would be 'open', and she would be like God, knowing good and evil. She would be able to choose, to decide for herself what was good and evil. No longer would that choice be made for her.

Until that time Adam and Eve had only known what was good, what God had commanded. They had done everything in obedience to his commands. Now they and all their descendants were to know evil. The first sin led to all the sins.

The idea that man can choose his own god is absurd. If there is a God, he is, and nothing that man says or does can make the slightest difference. If God made us, we cannot stand in judgement on him. Where did our judgement come from? If God made us, he is eternal; we are here today and gone tomorrow. Our knowledge is limited, our ability limited, we find it hard to learn, hard to communicate, harder still to co-operate. Yet we want to sit in judgement on the Creator of this fruitful and beautiful universe, with its seed-time and harvest, summer and winter, night and day, cold and heat. He created its vast variety of plant and animal life, its energy, whose ultimate source nobody knows nor can know, its fine balance of temperature, moisture and oxygen without which no human, animal or vegetable life is possible. We are just beginning to understand the mechanisms and systems of the universe, yet we behave as if we invented it all ourselves.

The ecologists are now telling us that we tamper with the balance of nature at our peril. The conservationists tell us that we must not squander its carefully stored energy, or poison the world with our crude short-cuts to cheap power. The god of science is not infallible. Human knowledge is dangerous if it is not subject to the moral commands of the Creator.

The failure of humanist solutions

It is equally arrogant for man to think that he can deal with the problem of evil on his own. Evil is a fact with which any religious belief has to come to terms. If we invent an evil god then we have to explain the existence of good. But if we believe, as Christians do, in the goodness of God, then we have to explain evil.

Christianity teaches that only the power of God can overcome evil. Human teaching is that evil can be overcome by the gods of our own invention. The Marxists believe that evil can be overcome by the correct Marxist policies, which will transform society, and remove the need for wrong-doing. Remove a greedy capitalism and greed itself will gradually vanish. If only this were true.

But even in the Western democracies, we are relying on sociology to do God's work. There is nothing wrong with sociology. It is important to understand the structure of society. For example it is better to have housing policies which support family life and improve the dignity of man than those which destroy the vital relationships which hold a community together. But, just as the physical sciences were arrogant enough to want to be a law to themselves, so are the social sciences.

The social worker cannot deal with the problem of evil. Evil will only be contained by a strong belief, at every level of society, in the moral law. There must be a healthy respect for the immediate, and ultimate, consequences of breaking it.

In the last twenty-five years we have experimented with humanist morality. We have arrogantly thrown over the Christian moral order, and with it, the basic disciplines which have curbed evil in all kinds of societies at most times in human history. Our generation has decided that social science could solve the problems of evil far better than Christian morality. It has pursued greater respect for human life. But murder has quadrupled, crimes of violence have increased nine times and one fifth of Britain's unborn babies are destroyed. In pursuit of greater human freedom and happiness, the security of family life has been shattered. A rootless and unloved generation is growing up restless, lonely and unhappy. In the pursuit of the liberation of women, divorce by consent has been introduced. It has removed the need for a man to care for a wife he has ceased to love. It has made the wife who wants to keep him into a slave who has to care for his every whim. It has placed the young family who need his income and protection into a more subservient position than that of any Victorian child in the hey-day of paternal power. And all because humanist sociology knew best.

There is more profound human misery around us than at any time in human memory. We have more money, better health, better education, greater social mobility. We have more democratic rights than ever before, and have enjoyed a long period of peace. Yet people are miserable, aimless, envious, mean and discontented. The god of humanist morality is failing.

The gods of Western civilization

But perhaps the greatest god of our age is materialism. What matters more to our generation than money? It is not the first time that men have made money their god. The apostle Paul wrote that the love of money was the root of all evil. But there have been times when other things seemed to matter more. In wartime men fight for freedom, and everybody is prepared to make sacrifices. In the Middle Ages, great cathedrals rose all over Europe. Maybe the money should have been spent on the poor; but there was a genuine religious feeling in society which expressed itself in this way. In other ages rank or power has mattered more than money.

Today money is supreme. Governments rise and fall according to the buying-power of a week's wages. Nothing else seems to matter. Economic success brings electoral reward; economic restraint brings electoral disaster. The big news in the papers is about the wage-packets. The big social conflicts are about money. Government coalitions stand or fall on five pence on the price of petrol. Interest in other people's earnings is intense. Envy of high earnings is ferocious.

Yet, like any false god, materialism destroys its worshippers. If governments have to bribe the electors to regain power, the electors will get what they ask for – money. But the money will be worth less and less with every election. For real wealth cannot be created in an atmosphere of rabid materialism. Real wealth needs restraint by consumers. It needs savings and investment.

The mad scramble for money eats up the nation's savings. It destroys industrial capital, and leads to poverty and unemployment. Governments are now beginning to despair of finding a way out. Money has become unstable. Real growth of wealth is much more difficult to achieve. Unemployment, especially among the young, is now an almost insoluble problem.

The false god of nationalism has plagued the twentieth century. The two World Wars have cost 50 million human lives. Twenty million Russians and six million Jews lost their lives in the four years between 1941 and 1945. Our contemporaries in Germany regret this as much as we do. They are no more to blame than we are. There is no doubt that a new generation has risen from the ashes, and Germany will not easily tread that path again.

Yet the commandment is true. The iniquities of the fathers are visited upon the children to the third and fourth generation. Berlin, the place from which those wars were ordered, is divided and ringed in steel. West Berlin is completely surrounded by a wall. It is guarded by machine-guns, triggered automatically to shoot to pieces anybody who crosses their firepath. The wall is backed by a fence, a free-fire zone, anti-vehicle obstacles, an electric fence, and a string of guard-posts, with alsatian dogs and searchlights.

East Berlin, which contains the old heart of the city, is now a ghost town. I have a book containing photographs of Berlin at the turn of the century. One shows the bustling junction of the *Unter den Linden* with the *Friederichstrasse*. It has news-stands – today there are no news-stands. It has two hotels – today there are none. It has shops – today there are none. It has trams – today no-body wants to travel there. Now at the end of the *Friederichstrasse* is 'Check-point Charlie'. Nearby was the Chancellery, where giants such as Bismark once presided. Today there is a mound of grass. At the other end of the *Unter den Linden*, the Kaiser's palace is no more. The cathedral is still torn by ugly scars from the war.

In and around modern Berlin are tanks, troops, missiles and, not far away, nuclear weapons. Other old photographs of that proudest of cities show the splendid buildings, monuments of national victory, and military reviews. The uniforms, the flags and the panoply of the great German Reich are all aglow with aggressive self-conscious nationalism. But look today at the city still occupied by foreign troops. It is divided and isolated on the barrier between East and West. It depends on others for its security, the focus of the tension it itself created in its hey-day. You cannot but think of the long drawn-out consequences of the sins of fathers on their children, and children's children.

But a visit to a communist city offers more than one contrast. It has no pornography, no strip-shows, no blue films, no sex shops. Communism is a puritanical culture. By contrast we can see how the democracies have made a god out of sex.

The sex-cult has gods and goddesses. It has the whole para-phernalia of worship, and a life-style to go with it. People expect of it, as they do of their gods, far more than they can give. When the excitement palls, addicts work themselves up into ever greater frenzies, with ever stronger stimulation.

We have only to stand back a little to see how absurd and destructive the whole mad process is. It destroys the very instinct on which it feeds with wild overstimulation. Finally sex, this tenderest of all instincts, is dead. There is nothing uniquely modern about this. Many ancient goddesses were surrounded by a similar sickly culture. Many ancient societies went to rot in the same way. The Old Testament itself tells us of some of them. Or, as the Latin tag says, 'Whom the gods wish to destroy, they first make mad.'

It is not everybody today who worships the goddess of sex. Some, in complete contrast, worship sport. Sport, like sex, has its place in a balanced life. But there are people who live for sport. There are racing drivers who know – if they think at all – that they are likely to die for their sport. I gave up going to motor-races over twenty years ago, when four drivers were killed in one race I was watching.

I enjoyed playing football, but I do not believe in worshipping a football team. I believe in healthy exercise. But I do not believe that we should be obsessed by the pursuit of a small, white ball round the countryside in the minimum number of strokes. Golf must not be to the exclusion of wife and children and all conversation about anything else afterwards. The same goes for hunting.

But there are more dangerous forms of worship. Some men worship power. They want power with all their being – and the fame that power brings with it. I have now spent over a dozen years in public life, and I have learnt to be very wary of the temptations of this god.

We can delude ourselves that we want power for the benefit of others, for our ideals, or for our children. But we enjoy power. We do not want to give it up. Democracy, however, depends on our willingness to give up power. It depends on our willingness to be ruled by those with whom we disagree. Democracy requires the willingness of the minority to be ruled by the majority. When the minority are unwilling, democracy breaks down. They justify violence arguing it is the only option when they cannot obtain what they ask by democratic means. The democrat's answer is to accept the rule of somebody with whom he disagrees, and try to influence fellow-citizens.

But the search for power is self-defeating. Those who take power by violence, lose power by violence. What everybody wants, nobody can have for long. Brief are the fruits of power. Frustrating is the exercise of power. Bitter – very bitter – is the loss of power to those who have wanted it above all else.

Changing people's minds will, in the end, change their actions. That is influence. It is hard work to exercise influence. But it lasts. To try to change people's actions without changing their minds is frustrating – and ultimately futile.

Devil worship

In the final analysis all false worship is futile. But some false worship is immediately and overtly evil. The ultimate in false worship is the worship of the devil himself. For hundreds of years Satanism has been banished from Britain. But in this so-called scientific age, which claims to have abolished belief in the devil, it is back with us again.

I was at a diocesan meeting where one lady was complaining that it was difficult to be distinctively Christian in a respectable society. Another woman stood up: 'Don't you believe it, my dear. We have thirteen witches' covens in our parish – and they're distinctively different!'

Witches' covens have multiplied. Spiritualism of all kinds has increased. People give themselves over to worship evil spirits, to obey their commands, even to be possessed by them. Christians are having to learn all over again about the gifts, and hazards, of exorcism. Foolish men, who know nothing of the whole perilous business, are attributing the evil to the attempted cure. They imagine that there is no possession until cure is attempted.

Missionaries know the terrors of this kind of worship. They attest to its reality and its violent destructive force. And its return to Britain shows how far we have fallen. But at least it alerts us to the reality of the unseen world. It should drive us back to the true God, who has the power to curb and control evil.

When we were in Singapore in 1978, my wife and I met Bishop Ban It Chiu, and Professor Khoo, of the Medical Faculty of the University of Singapore. They have dealt with a great many cases of demon-possession. They have to diagnose negatively that it is not a medical case, and positively that there is an evil spirit.

They once exorcised a girl who turned out to be possessed by no less than six evil spirits. One of these tried to bargain:

'Cast me into the girl next-door. She is unclean.' 'No, you must go out into the abyss.' 'Cast me into the dog.' 'No you must go into the abyss.' Finally the last spirit went, and the girl was free.

They told us that the spirits seem to come in through some interest by the possessed person – or by a member of their close family – in the occult. Often they come in through the purchase on nearby islands of idol masks or fetish symbols. The exorcists destroy such articles. But, like others who practise exorcism, they said that it is difficult and dangerous for everybody involved. It should never be undertaken by those who are unqualified and unauthorized.

The power of evil spirits can be countered by the power of Christ. But meantime, their power is terrifyingly real and horribly inhuman. We heard these accounts from the Bishop across the dinner table of the British High Commissioner. The High Commissioner's wife was apalled. 'I had no idea such things went on in Singapore.'

The exclusiveness of Christianity
God tolerates no rivals. He alone made us. He alone gave us all we have. He requires that our allegiance shall be to him alone.

The false prophets of our day deny that there is one true God, and no other. Nobody who claims to be a Christian can deny it. The Christian faith is exclusive. It does not admit another faith. It is not part of the truth. Christianity is *the* truth. Jesus said: I am the way, the truth and the life. No man comes to the father but by me.' Paul told the Christians at Corinth: 'There is no God but one' and 'For us there is one God, the Father, from whom are all things, and for whom we exist, and one Lord, Jesus Christ, through whom are all things, and through whom we exist.' Paul wrote to the Thessalonian Christians: 'You turned to God from idols, to serve a living and true God.'

Elsewhere the apostle describes God as: 'God only wise.'
Or listen to the Psalmist:
'Our God is in the heavens;
    he does whatever he pleases.
Their idols are silver and gold,
    the work of men's hands.
They have mouths, but do not speak;

eyes, but do not see.
They have ears, but do not hear;
    noses, but do not smell.
They have hands, but do not feel;
    feet, but do not walk;
    and they do not make a sound in their throat.
Those who make them are like them;
    so are all who trust in them.
O Israel, trust in the Lord!
    He is their help and their shield.'

It is the Lord who made us. He knows us, one by one. It is he to whom we must answer. It is this Lord who came as man to die for us. He died for all our sins, including our worship of other gods. He asks us simply to trust in his death for the forgiveness of our sins. He alone will receive those who repent and are forgiven, to live with him forever.

So, whether we are Christians or not, we should examine our lives. What are our own idols? What are we living for? Work? Is our professional reputation our god? Do we live for our life-style? Do we live for sport? Do we have Saturday-night fever? Would we do most things for money?

I once asked a friend with whom I rowed to come to a church service. My request broke our friendship. He lived for rowing, and stayed at university an extra year, simply to row. Then he contracted polio and was crippled for life. His god betrayed him – as in the end all false gods betray those who worship them.

Chapter 3

What's in a name?

You shall not take the name of the Lord your God in vain;
for the Lord will not hold him guiltless who takes his
name in vain.

It is odd in this so-called secular age, when so few people believe in God, that the name of God is always on their lips. If there is no God, what is the point of cursing God? And yet everybody does it.

But for those of us who do believe in God, the reason is clear. It just shows that there is, in everybody, an instinctive belief in God, and an instinctive rebellion against him.

For all those old-fashioned swearwords we use are, in fact, a litany of rebellion. They are the angry shorthand for a long list of complaints we have against the God who made us. They express our hate for our fellow men and women, whom God tells us to love. They mark our disrespect for the God who commands our respect, and for our fellow men who, like us, are made in his image.

Blasphemy is the exact opposite of all God tells us to do and to say. It has a theology all of its own. It is not indifferent. It is antagonism so exact and detailed that it reflects the positive nature of the Being against which it is directed. Blasphemy detracts, first of all, from the honour of God. Honour is not highly thought of today. But it is an idea quite common to man.

The Jubilee service at St Paul's Cathedral was held to honour the Queen for twenty-five years' service to Britain and the Commonwealth. It was an elaborate affair. It was held in a fine cathedral, with a great organ, a well-practised choir and splendid trumpeters. The Queen was protected by her Gentlemen-at-Arms and the Beefeaters. The heads of all the orders of chivalry were on parade. All her family came, together with her prime ministers, the ambassadors of every country in which her government was represented, and two thousand British citizens from every walk of life.

Half-a-million people turned out to see her procession and a hundred thousand stood outside her palace at the end. I do not like to think of the fate of anybody, inside or outside the cathedral, who had voiced criticism on that day. Yet a queen is only human. Blasphemy against the glory of God is of a wholly different order.

The splendour of God

God has given something of this glory to the men and women he has made. We are made in his image. So to curse men made in the image of God is to detract from the glory of God himself.

To take the human analogy again, any hurt to the Queen's subjects is a hurt to the Queen. It is an offence which her judges must notice and remedy. But we are not merely God's subjects, we are his creation. The relationship of mankind to God, our relationships to each other, have been thought out and put in order by God. To destroy the harmony of those relationships is to destroy what God himself has made.

So to curse our fellow men and women is to fly in the face of God Almighty. It is to wish them ill when God wishes them good. It is to wish them damned when God wishes them saved. It is to despise them when God respects them. It is to hate them when God loves them and has died for them. Curses may be no more than words to us. But words reflect an attitude so strong that it must find expression. They betray a hostility so deep we cannot prevent it bursting out.

The world today does not believe in the Creator. So it does not believe in his glory and power. Yet the glory and power of God is seen in the beauty of creation. If we really believed that there was no creator, we would be hard put to it to explain beauty. If everything in the world is an accident, then a field of daffodils is as much an accident as a slag-heap.

The Bible is full of awe at the greatness and glory of God, and the beauty of his creation. Read the Psalms:

'The heavens are telling the glory of God;
And the firmament proclaims his handiwork.'
'When I look at thy heavens, the work of thy fingers,
   the moon and the stars which thou hast established;
What is man that thou art mindful of him,
   and the son of man that thou dost care for him?

Thou hast given him dominion over the works of thy hands;
   thou hast put all things under his feet.'
Or take God's own words to Job:
   'Where were you when I laid the foundation of the earth?
      Tell me, if you have understanding.
   Who determined its measurements — surely you know!
      Or who stretched the line upon it?
   On what were its bases sunk,
      Or who laid its cornerstone,
   when the morning stars sang together, and all the sons of
      God shouted for joy?'
And so it continues for two magnificent chapters, ending with
the question:
   'Shall a faultfinder contend with the Almighty?
      He who argues with God, let him answer it.'
Job is overcome. He says:
   'Behold, I am of small account;
      What shall I answer thee?
   I lay my hand on my mouth.
   I have spoken once, and I will not answer;
      twice, but I will proceed no further.'
Job's temptation was to curse God for his misfortunes. He
would not yield. But he still could see no justice in his
misfortunes. God tells him:
   'Gird up your loins like a man;
      I will question you, and you shall declare to me.
   Will you even put me in the wrong?
      Will you condemn me that you may be justified?'
God goes on to contrast his power and glory with the men who
questioned him:
   'Who has given to me, that I should repay him?
   Whatever is under the whole heaven is mine.'
Finally Job says:
   'I have uttered what I did not understand . . .
   therefore I despise myself, and repent in dust and ashes.'

   The Bible is also full of stories of people who have been
overcome by a sight of the greatness and glory of God. Isaiah
tells us: 'In the year that King Uzziah died I saw the Lord
sitting upon a throne, high and lifted up; and his train filled the
temple . . . And I said: "Woe is me! For I am lost; for I am a
man of unclean lips, and I dwell in the midst of a people of

unclean lips; for my eyes have seen the King, the Lord of Hosts!"'

Notice that Job says, 'I lay my hand on my mouth.' Isaiah says: 'I am a man of unclean lips.' When we become conscious of the glory of God, it is our words which we regret before our deeds.

Let us go to the New Testament, to Matthew's account of Christ's transfiguration before Peter, James and John: 'His face shone like the sun, and his garments became white as light.' While Peter was speaking 'a bright cloud overshadowed them, and a voice from the cloud said, "This is my beloved Son, with whom I am well pleased; listen to him." When the disciples heard this, they fell on their faces, and were filled with awe. But Jesus came and touched them, saying "Rise, and have no fear."'

We all know of the apostle Paul's encounter on the road to Damascus. He was Saul the Pharisee, persecuting the church. 'Suddenly a light from heaven flashed about him. And he fell to the ground and heard a voice saying to him, "Saul, Saul, why do you persecute me?" And he said "Who are you Lord?" And he said "I am Jesus, whom you are persecuting, but rise and enter the city and you will be told what you are to do."' Saul the persecutor obeyed. He became Paul the apostle to the Gentiles.

The apostle John had a second encounter with the glory of God. When he was on the island of Patmos he saw somebody like a son of man. 'His face was like the sun shining in full strength. When I saw him,' says John, 'I fell at his feet as though dead. But he laid his right hand upon me and said "Fear not, I am the first and the last, and the living one; I died and behold I am alive for evermore, and I have the keys of Death and Hades."'

Look at the effect of God's glory on those who believe in him. John also describes the effect of God's glory on those who do not trust him. 'Then the kings of the earth and the great men and the generals and the rich and the strong, and every one, slave and free, hid in the caves and among the rocks of the mountains, calling to the mountains and rocks, "Fall on us and hide us from the face of him who is seated on the throne, and from the wrath of the Lamb; for the great day of their wrath has come, and who can stand before it?"'

Notice that they cannot stand in the sight of God's holiness and glory. But they do not repent. They try to hide from God. But God does not tolerate those who blaspheme him. Wherever they rise, he will put them down and punish them. The faithful will be preserved.

That is the Christian picture of the glory of God. It shows the effect of the glory of God on the faithful, and on blasphemers. It invokes the judgement of God for those who do not repent of their blasphemies. It is an awesome picture.

The love and justice of God

The problem of our own day is that we refuse to be awed by anything or anybody. Everything is trivialized, explained away in comfortable terms. The TV newcaster explains disasters in terms which are acceptable at the fireside. Fake corpses litter the screen, but real ones are edited out. Horror is sent up on the late-night movies. God is reduced to a subject for panel discussion, on which men and women sit in judgement.

The idea that God might sit in judgement on us is not admitted for a moment. The idea of punishment by a holy God for blasphemy is not even discussed. Modern thinking is against divine punishment – so there cannot be any.

But let us take our minds away for a moment from modern ideas. Imagine, for the sake of argument, that God *did* create this great universe. Stretch the imagination just a little, to conceive of a being who is greater than we are, and holy and just. Then begin to imagine God's attitude towards those who having received everything from him, will give nothing. Those who will not talk of him except in terms of hostility, hatred and contempt. Even our common sense might warn us that this is an unwise attitude to one so powerful; that such defiance is unlikely to last long.

But, says modern man, God is love. However bad we are, a God of love is bound to forgive us. Now of course it is true that God is love. But God is also just. God cannot live with open rebellion; nor can open rebellion live with God.

We cannot dictate to Almighty God the way to justice and his love. He has chosen his own way, and we have to accept it. God's way is to bear the punishment of sin himself, in the person of God the Son. He loved us so much, despite our sin and rebellion, that he sent his Son to die for us. Christ accepted the punishment for sin, which is physical death and separation

from God. As he died on the cross, God separated himself from
the Son. The Son cried: 'My God, My God, why have you
forsaken me?'

God accepted this sacrifice. The sign that he did so is
Christ's resurrection from the dead. The resurrection was
witnessed by the apostles and many of the disciples. For only
God, who gives life, can give a new life. There is no grave of
Jesus Christ.

Where does this leave those who are hostile to God? It
makes them hostile not only to God their Creator, but also to
God their Redeemer. They are hostile not only to the God of
justice, but also to the God of love. Those who maintain their
hostility in the face of God's love make their rebellion ten times
worse. For surrender to God no longer means punishment; it
means forgiveness.

And God not only has an exalted and remote position as our
Creator. He has himself taken our humanity. Nor has he come
to earth as king; he came to earth as a common man. He did
not come to earth to judge. He came to be judged, to suffer and
to die. He did not come to die for those who loved him, he came
to die for those who hated him. He did not respond to *our*
overtures. He made the advances. He asks us to respond to
him.

Those who are hostile cannot bear this moral pressure, the
pressure of love freely and sacrificially given. They do not
want to owe anything to God. They want to earn their own
way to heaven. But the door of heaven has no handle on the
outside. There is no other way to heaven. Jesus said 'I am the
way, and the truth, and the life. No one comes to the Father
except through me.'

Had there been any other way, God the Son would not have
had to suffer and die. To talk of 'other ways' is to belittle the
sacrifice of God the Son. It is to say that it was irrelevant and
unnecessary. It is to put somebody or something else in
Christ's place as the way to God. And that is blasphemy. But
many people want human efforts to figure somewhere in their
plan of salvation. Whatever Christ has done, they want to feel
that they have done something too.

The apostle Paul puts it plainly and precisely in his letter to
the Ephesians. 'For by grace you have been saved through
faith; and this is not your own doing it is a gift of God – not
because of works, lest any man should boast.' To think that we

can add to what Christ has done is to detract from the work of Christ. It puts our efforts on a level with his works, and that too is blasphemy.

Respect for human dignity

The first commandment is to love God with all our heart, and mind, and soul, and strength. Christ added that the second was like it; that we should love our neighbour as ourselves. These two commands, said Christ, summed up all the law and the prophets. The first command leads on to the second. If we do not keep the first command, we find that we do not keep the second. If we are hostile to God, we will be hostile to our fellow men. If we curse God, we will find ourselves cursing man made in the image of God. If we hate God, we will find ourselves hating our fellow men.

To turn again to the apostle John, 'If any one says "I love God," and hates his brother, he is a liar, for he who does not love his brother whom he has seen, cannot love God whom he has not seen.'

The first command and the second command are tied tightly together. It is the heresy of secular society to think that they can be separated. Our link with our fellow men is God, who made us both. Cut that link with God, and we cut the link with our fellow men. Blasphemy against our fellow men and women is blasphemy against God who made them. God knows each of them. Every single man and woman is personally accountable to God for all they do and say.

There is a whole language of blasphemy which aims to degrade men and women. It reduces them to the level of animals. It identifies them entirely with the grossest behaviour. It strips them of any decency, respect, dignity or honour. We would hardly address a dog in such a way – it would not seem worthwhile.

Why is there in us this urge to destroy the dignity of people? We cannot claim that it is just words and nobody should take much notice. Words reflect attitudes, and attitudes lead to actions. Listen to Jesus, in the Sermon on the Mount: 'You have heard that it was said to the men of old, "You shall not kill; and whoever kills shall be liable to judgement." But I say to you that everyone who is angry with his brother shall be liable to the council, and whoever says, "You fool!" shall be liable to the hell of fire.'

Christ was pointing out that sin is within. It is an attitude as much as an action. We must not treat our fellow men and women as fools. We are bound to respect them. It is this respect which leads to government by consent. It is contempt of the common man and woman which leads to tyranny. It is respect for every citizen, however humble, which leads to the rule of law, and equality before the law. It is a lack of respect which leads to the arbitrary and partial justice of the police state, where nobody is certain of his rights, and there is no appeal.

It is respect for the individual which leads to education for all, and to the dissolving of class-barriers. It is lack of respect which leads to the belief that some classes and some races are beyond help, and not worth educating. It is respect for all men which inspires us to apply our energy to reducing poverty, to creating the physical conditions in which men and women can live in dignity. It inspires the attempt to provide employment for all, so that nobody suffers the degradation of being thrown on the scrap-heap, his contribution unwanted.

Marxists and humanists share many of these ideals with Christians. But they have no theology, and ideals must have a theology. If they have to be imposed they cease to be ideals, they become just another tyranny. As awe for God has dimmed, so has our respect for our fellow men. Violence and hatred are on the increase. So is the language of blasphemy, which expresses the hatred and envy which simmer inside us.

Christians must show their love for God and for their fellow men in word and deed. We must guard our attitudes and our tongues. The Bible says, 'The tongue is a fire. The tongue is an unrighteous world among our members, staining the whole body, setting on fire the cycle of nature, and set on fire by hell.'

Not every wrong use of God's name is hostile. There are those who try to tap its power. The sons of a Jew called Sceva tried to use the name of 'Jesus whom Paul preaches' for an illicit exorcism. The evil spirit answered them 'Jesus I know and Paul I know, but who are you?' Then the man who had the evil spirit jumped on them and overpowered them. He gave them such a beating that they ran out of the house naked and bleeding.

Formal oaths
The most common use of the name of God has been to

reinforce a man's own word. In our literate society a signature affirms our decision. If the decision is important, the signature is witnessed by one or two other people. In an illiterate society the oath is much more important. We find oaths throughout the Old Testament. Many of the most important are oaths on God's name.

An oath calls God to witness that what we say is true. To swear it implies that we believe that God exists, that he can hear, that he is just and powerful, that he governs the world, that we are accountable to him for our actions. If we do not believe in any one of these, then there is no point in swearing before God. To do so in disbelief is to take God's name in vain. Obviously to tell a lie on oath before God is also to use his name in vain.

There have been Christians from time to time, such as the Quakers, who have taken Christ's words 'Swear not at all' as a complete prohibition of oaths of any kind. This caused them endless trouble in magistrates' courts, before witnesses were allowed to affirm as an alternative to an oath.

But Christ did not put himself in opposition to Moses Law – indeed he supported it. Moses says that in a dispute about animals in a neighbour's care, 'an oath by the Lord shall be between them both . . . and the owner shall accept the oath'. What Christ was attacking in the Sermon on the Mount was oaths which sounded solemn – such as an oath by heaven, by the earth or by Jerusalem – but which the swearers would say could not be blasphemous, because they did not mention God's name. He points out that all three are connected with God. There is no need to bring such oaths into conversation for emphasis, where a straight 'Yes' and 'No' will do perfectly well.

But there do seem to be occasions when a solemn oath is necessary. Paul told the Roman Christians, 'God is my witness how constantly I remember you in my prayers at all times.' He told the Corinthian Christians, 'I call God as my witness that it was in order to spare you that I did not return to Corinth.'

It has generally been held by Christians that oaths must be for solemn occasions. For instance there is an oath of allegiance to a head of state, or an inaugural oath by a head of state in countries with a constitution recognizing the Christian church. If it is 'assertive', like Paul's two oaths quoted above, it must be on an ocassion which really required a solemn oath like a formal letter to a church. To use other oaths on God's name, meant for the most solemn occasions, to reinforce a point in casual conversation, is to belittle the whole process of a solemn oath. It belittles God's name.

A society which does not believe in God is not impressed with oaths in God's name. The secular state has ceased to rely on the oath. It is more impressed with the lie-detector. But within our lifetime the wheel may turn full circle. Christians may find themselves in the same anxiety as Christians in the German army, who had to swear an oath of allegiance to their head of state, Adolf Hitler. The answer to them, and to others like them, is that an oath, like the command to a child to obey its parents, is only binding so long as it binds us to do something lawful. We cannot bind ourselves before God to do something which God prohibits.

The validity of vows
The same is true of vows. Like oaths, these are not in vogue in our permissive society. But as people cease to believe each other, and promises need hard support, oaths and vows may soon be with us again.

The Protestants argued at the Reformation that vows of celibacy were not binding, because they were vows to remain in a condition which God had not ordained for men and women. Martin Luther, the reforming monk, took a wife, Catherine, and had a family. On the other hand, the marriage vow — now the most common of vows — was, and still is, regarded as binding, because God had ordained marriage. A church which recognizes the validity of marriage vows as taken before God cannot, without breaking the third commandment, go through the same ceremony, with the same vows, with those who are breaking their previous vows.

Chapter 4

A day with a difference

*Remember the sabbath day, to keep it holy. Six days you
shall labour, and do all your work; but the seventh day is
a sabbath to the Lord your God; in it you shall not do any
work, you, or your son, or your daughter, your manservant,
or your maidservant, or your cattle, or the sojourner who is
within your gates; for in six days the Lord made heaven
and earth, the sea, and all that is in them, and rested the
seventh day; therefore the Lord blessed the sabbath day
and hallowed it.*

For most of the history of the human race, and in most of the
world today, life is a grinding toil, with long hours and low
wages. The complete release from work for one day in seven is
a vital protection to health and strength. It is absolutely
necessary as protection to the working man and woman.
However hard they work for six days, they must be set free on
the seventh. The human frame was not made to stand
unending work. Rest at night is imposed by darkness. Rest on
the seventh day is ordered by God.

The institution of the sabbath restrains the exploitation of
labour. It is a social law to protect the worker. Even in today's
irreligious society, the trades unions would be the first to
protest if Sunday were treated like any other day. If an
employer insists that work has to be done on Sunday, it costs
him double the hourly rate. This is a strong incentive to avoid
Sunday work.

The reduction of the working week to five days has obscured
the special protection of Sunday. But it is still trades union
policy to have one day when all but essential services cease.
There would be stormy protests from the trades union movement against the general introduction of Sunday shopping. So
there is more support for the social aim of the sabbath, even
today, than we might realize.

The one day off in seven is also meant to protect us from
ourselves. There are those who find it hard to organize their
time, and there are also those who are chronic workers. They
want to make money or they are obsessed by their job. Such
people include the executive or professional worker who, when
he comes home, either works or sleeps from exhaustion.

In professional life today many people take work home. They put it aside during the week for work over the weekend. So instead of a father being free for his wife and children, he is buried in his work. The problems of the business or profession never cease. At no point does the worker get a clear break. That is bad for him, bad for his work, and especially bad for his wife and family. It is the cause of executive stress, and puts an unnecessary strain on marriage. The self-employed also find it hard to stop working.

The Jews have always been great men of business. In biblical times, no sooner had Nehemiah rebuilt the city walls of Jerusalem, than they were holding markets, buying and selling on every available day, right through the week. So Nehemiah ordered that the doors of the city be closed on the sabbath. Even then merchants hung about outside the gates, and he had to warn them off.

In a commercial community, the closing of the market has to be general. If the market is kept open for some, they will secure an advantage. And since it is unlikely that more business will be transacted in seven days than in six, no harm is done if everybody takes one day off.

There is a natural rhythm in life which demands complete relaxation between periods of effort. The athlete, and others who push physical effort and mental concentration to its extreme points of endurance, know this very well. An oarsman relaxes completely as he comes forward for his next stroke.

Our tense, preoccupied urban society has lost this ability to switch off. With this loss has gone the loss of the natural rhythm of life. The reason we read a lot in the papers of the need to relax is that people have lost the ability to relax. They drive themselves to hypertension and breakdown. The Christian – and Jewish – insistence on one day in seven completely removed from our daily preoccupations gives the rest and rhythm which we need to meet the stresses and strains of life today.

But the seventh day is not meant to be a vacuum, a long, boring day when nothing happens. Man is spirit as well as body. The sabbath is a time when we remember that there is more to life than buying and selling. We remind ourselves that there is a meaning to life, that each of us matters, and that we are not just a number on a wage-packet and a pension-scheme.

A time for reflection

The Christian and the man of the world may agree this far. The Christian may persuade others that Sunday makes physical and psychological good sense. But to the man of the world the break means the golf-course, the pub, the trip in the car, the garden, or friends to dinner. The idea of dressing up and going to church seems too boring to contemplate. And there is no doubt that churches which go through the ritual of a service without any spirit, life or relevant message are very boring.

But the Christian church is not meant to be like that. It is meant to stimulate. It is meant to challenge conventional wisdom and to put our everyday world into perspective. It is intended to help us to take a different view, to look at ourselves as spiritual beings, made in the image of God the Creator. If our church life is not like that, it should be.

Man without God is only half a man. We were made for a relationship with God, and without that relationship something is missing. So life without God is empty. No wonder modern man feels that life is meaningless, that people are so unhappy, that modern philosophy is despairing.

Christians are as capable of enjoying weekend sport as anybody else. They enjoy motoring and gardening. But they know they need something more. Over the years I have seen men so dedicated to their eighteen holes of golf on Sunday morning, that church-going was ruled out completely. I worked with a head clerk once who could not possibly go to church, because Sunday lunch was, as far as I could make out, his major event of the week. I know other people equally dedicated to Sunday fishing.

But I see life slipping away from the Sunday golfer. His job is coming to an end. His wife has left him. His children can only take him in small doses. How is his golf going to help him to come to terms with that? These recreations elevated into small gods, cannot help us to deal with the problems of life – let alone with the problem of death.

Without God, man is missing his most vital faculty, spiritual sight. He lacks the most vital support, the warmth of divine love. Here on this one day in the week, is a reminder that God is waiting for us to come to him. We can listen to what he has to say, find out how we can be at one with him and find our spiritual sight. For the first time we can become full human beings – body, soul and spirit.

A place to find God

Christians understand the prejudice against going to church. There was a time when they felt it themselves, even if only as children. I shall never forget the utter tedium of the services our family used to attend. They lasted an hour-and-a-half, and there was no piano or organ. Any male member could speak or pray. Many were inarticulate working men who, though they felt passionately, were quite unable to put their feelings into words. The result was a series of disconnected and resounding cliches, which meant nothing to me at all.

School chapel was at the other extreme. A series of highly intelligent preachers apologized articulately for a faith they no longer seemed to hold. Bets were made on the number of times the headmaster would remove his glasses. However inarticulate the working men, I learnt more from them than from the chaplains. I learnt that the Christian faith could change the most unlikely people, that it was not just a part of the British establishment. I shall never forget the prayer of a big policeman who had just lost his wife. He knew that she was in heaven. No one could doubt the depth of the faith which held him in his bereavement.

It is the people who make a church – not the stained-glass windows. There is more life in many a tin tabernacle than in the greatest cathedral. The cathedral is a museum. True it embodies a worship in stone which is breath-takingly magnificent, and makes us stop to think. It also embodies the continuity of the Christian faith down the years. And it can contain a lively congregation. You can have a church without a building, but you cannot have a church without Christians.

So it is worth persisting in the effort to find a church whose members clearly believe the faith that they profess, and show it in the welcome they give to the stranger. But the faith should be backed by intelligent teaching from the pulpit, explaining what God's word means in terms which we can understand today. We should not stay too long with a preacher whose sermons give his own personal view on life and politics. There is no reason why his view should be better than ours. It is unlikely to be better informed than the leader in the Sunday paper which we can read in comfort at home.

Recently, my wife and I went to a church in California where we listened to the minister give half-an-hour's straight-forward explanation of a New Testament story to a congregation of three thousand. This was the second of three Sunday morning services. He was not imposing his own personal views, he was letting God's word speak with its own authority. This is why his Sunday morning service was full, and ran for three shifts, attended by nine thousand worshippers in all.

Some people go to church for the atmosphere, some for the music. Some – though it must be a small minority today – because it is respectable. Some mistakenly think that the ritual of going to church somehow balances off their wrongdoing through the week. But the first purpose in going to church is to find God.

We can read about Christianity in books. But to discover whether what we read is valid, we have to meet the people who profess the faith, and try to live by it. The Christian faith is best understood and judged by personal encounter. If it is what it claims to be, then it should change the lives of its adherents. This change should show in relationships to each other, and to strangers when they meet together. If there is any power of 'new life', it should be evident to the visitor. So it is worth going to the church to have a look.

There are countries where it is not so easy to go to church. In some countries it is forbidden. In other one-party states, with no legal political opposition, governments worry about the one country-wide organization which can command widespread loyalty, and which could become a substitute opposition. They watch it like a hawk, discouraging it as much as they dare. They react at the slightest sign that the church is trespassing into the political arena. Yet a higher proportion of people go to church in these countries than go in Western Europe, where there is real freedom of religion.

I once asked a Filipino student on a UN scholarship to a university in one such country how many people there were in his church on a Sunday. He said there were 800, with 400 and 600 in the other two Protestant churches and an equivalent number in the Catholic churches. He said that, although it was put about that only the working-class went to church, this was not true. There were a lot of professional people in his church too. He added that he had attended a service in a British cathedral and there had only been three or four families. He thought it was a tragedy that nobody in Britain went to church any longer. We have fought for freedom to worship in this country, and we have not had it for long. We should take advantage of it while we have it.

A community of encouragement

For the Christians especially Sunday's centre should be the church. We are told by the writer of the Letter to the Hebrews 'Let us consider how to stir up one another to love and good works, not neglecting to meet together, as is the habit of some but encouraging one another.'

This does not mean merely attending a service, a duty to be done. We are not doing something which will bring a *mechanical* benefit. This is God's day, the day on which we thank God for all he has done. A service is an act of worship. The free churches, rightly, lay great stress on the sermon – but worship is not such a strong point. We would do well to see that our worship reflects both our depth of feeling to God our Redeemer, and our awe of God the Creator. Our worship should never be dreary. It should always be lively, fresh, and yet reverent.

We can worship anywhere – in an upper room or a mud hut. But if we ourselves live in brightly-painted, comfortable houses, people take note if we meet in dingy, dilapidated and uncomfortable churches. If our worship is to honour and remember God, our Saviour and Creator, we should honour him in the place of worship too.

We come together to 'stir up one another to love and good works' and to 'encourage one another'. Sermons can do this. But sermons are to teach, and the writer to Hebrews seems to be talking of something which arises out of conversation and fellowship. In our own church in the centre of London we find it best to make a day of it. As a result we all get to know each other very well. We have time over meals, and between services and other meetings to talk and to spur each other on, and encourage one another.

Some people feel that all this is too much of a good thing. But it does produce a church which is a real community. Those who need help can find it. Young and old, and members from very different jobs and backgrounds, can knock the corners off each other, within the security of a lasting and friendly relationship. In a society criss-crossed with divisions of class, education, income, race, and age, this time spent together produces a rare and precious understanding of other points of view. It does not, of course, produce a perfect church. But it does help to solve some of the problems which face most churches.

A city-centre church – especially one in the middle of a capital city – is of course different. It usually has an influx of down-and-outs, and a constant stream of strangers. The close fellowship of Sunday cannot become a closed society. Indeed the stream of visitors is one reason for being in the church for the whole of Sunday. It is easy to ask visitors coming to London to drop in to see us there. Sundays are never dull!

Clarifying the message

The Christian messsage is both rich and relevant. It has within it the answer to the agonizing problems faced by everybody at some time or another. So it is vital that the message of the church, Sunday by Sunday, is not narrow. If the fourth commandment says that all mankind should keep one day holy to their Creator, then we owe it to them not to make the church services a barrier to their observance of the commandment.

The message preached each Sunday should be comprehensible to every generation. It should not be put in words or phrases which can only be understood by the seasoned churchgoer. Many organizations develop a language which only initiates can understand. The atmosphere makes the outsider *feel* an outsider. The church must never be like that. The truth should not be watered down. But it should be clear.

Those of us who speak to both Christian and non-Christian audiences are forced to consider the knowledge, assumptions and reasoning of our audiences. Each time we speak, we have to consider where we are, what our audience know and believe, and how we can best make ourselves clear to them. What words will they understand? What will grip them? What is likely to lose them or alienate them unnecessarily?

I am not advocating that we depart from Christian truth. But, like our Lord, we should speak in the images, similes, and terms our audiences can readily understand. There is enough difficulty in accepting the Christian message without adding unnecessary problems.

There are, understandably, Christians who react strongly against the attempts of some ministers to get people into church by any and every means, turning services into concerts. But there is no need to go to the other extreme. What we need is balance. Above all, Sunday services demand time and trouble. And those cost money. The world, in its wisdom, judges other people's dedication to a cause by the amount they are prepared to invest.

A means test for commitment

Money does not buy everything. But if we do not give the minimum required to our church, we are not doing all we can. We are not entitled to ask God to honour our efforts if we do not honour his command. That command is to give one tenth of our income. 'It is holy to the Lord.' He read in the Book of Malachi: 'Bring the full tithes into the storehouse, that there may be food in my house; and thereby put me to the test, says the Lord of hosts, if I will not open the windows of heaven for you and pour down for you an overflowing blessing.' Those who have given one tenth to God have invariably found that the nine-tenths remaining goes further than the whole amount previously. If we give God what he asks, he will give us what we need – and more.

Do not be mean. Do not start making deductions for tax – those are the expenses the state pays on our behalf. God is not mean. He is generous with those who are generous with him. If we have any faith, we should put it to the test. 'Try me,' says God. None of us is too poor. None of us is too highly taxed – the British government allows deduction of tax at the standard rate for covenanted income and other countries have similar arrangements. We can all try God.

A New Zealand friend believed when he started in business on his own that he should give not only a tenth, but proportionately more, if and when his income grew. It was not easy at the beginning to find both the tenth and the money to finance the business. But he persisted. He did so well that eventually over half his income went to Christian work.

Not every business genius is a Christian; not every Christian is a business genius. But the discipline of finding the tenth makes us take a lot more care of our money. We are less likely to waste it on useless extravagances. And the sense of God's partnership in our income gives us a much greater sense of responsibility in earning it. We cannot use unfair means of getting an income in partnership with God. And we cannot throw away potential income lightheartedly because it is not entirely our own.

So the practice of tithing builds a much greater care of income and expenditure. That is why we find that the ninety per cent goes further. But above and beyond this, God has his own ways of providing. There are times when all of us feel that we cannot afford the tithe – the poor because they are poor; the middle-class because inflation has reduced their spendable income; and the higher paid because tax takes five-sixths of any cost-of-living increase. Yet those who put God to the test find that they can trust him.

Double pay for clergy

We complain that people no longer come to church. Yet what do we do to encourage them? Do we respect our churches by keeping them cold, draughty, old-fashioned, with hard pews and dingy decoration? Does it look as if we take our faith seriously? In a materialistic age, people judge our seriousness by the amount of money we are prepared to spend. And how can anyone take our message seriously if we keep in poverty those we pay to give it?

Paul told Timothy that 'the elders who direct the affairs of the church well are worthy of double honour, especially those whose work is preaching and teaching'. He makes it clear that he is talking not just about respect, but about expressing the respect in terms of money. For the scripture says 'Do not muzzle the ox while it is treading out the grain' and 'The worker deserves his wages.' So if we are to honour our clergy and ministers, we should pay them double-time, or twice the average income of the congregation. We should see that their house and car match this.

There are churches that rely entirely on lay-preachers. But the church needs people who can give it their full attention. If a church tithes, then it only needs thirty wage-earners to pay double honour, and leave enough for heating and lighting. With sixty wage-earners, it should be able to afford a full-time assistant.

If the Christian message is all we say it is, then surely we want to give our preachers and teachers time to study it, to prepare adequate sermons and lectures. We want to attract the best young Christians to go into the church. Maybe they are so dedicated that they are prepared to serve on a starvation diet. Maybe – like Paul – they prefer to earn their income by making tents. But Paul laid down the principle, 'The Lord has commanded that those who preach the gospel should receive their living of the gospel'. They should not be driven out to secular occupations. They certainly should not be forced to live off their wives' incomes. Most certainly they should not have to apply to the state for national assistance.

Paul tells them later on, 'On the first day of the week each one of you should set aside a sum of money in keeping with his income, saving it up.' The principle of putting aside the proportion of our income as we earn it into a separate, sacrosanct, account is sound. Then God's account at the bank is secure against our extravagance. Paul does not leave it at that. In his second letter to the Corinthians, he tells them how to set about their giving. It should be planned it advance. It should be generous: 'Whoever sows sparingly will reap sparingly, and whoever sows generously will also reap generously.' It should be given generously 'for God loves a cheerful giver'. God will care for those who give, and remind them that their gift is a way of thanking God for his own indescribable gift.

The hard test of giving as God has commanded is one way of sorting out those who have a true Christian faith from those who are just playing at it. As James puts it in his letter to the churches, illustrating the link between faith and works, 'What good is it my brothers if a man claims to have faith but has no deeds? Can such faith save him? Suppose a brother or sister is without clothes and daily food. If one says to him "Go, I wish you well; keep warm and well fed", but does nothing about his physical needs, what good is it? In the same way, faith by itself, if it is not accompanied by action, is dead.'

Money enables us to send a promising younger man to study for the ministry. It also enables a full-time minister to study. It puts the Christian ministry on the same level as any other profession, and it enables us to have far more people who can use their talent, full-time and part-time.

If we honour God with our money, he will honour us with a ministry of which we will not be ashamed. That ministry will bring people to church on Sundays because they want to come. They will find there is a richness of thought and a wisdom which everybody needs in this barren, selfish and hopeless generation.

Money enables us to brighten the church buildings, to add

on halls and kitchens. We can buy vans to bring old folk to services and to collect children for Sunday school. Money helps to build a library of books and a library of tapes, places where people can sit to read the books and booths with head-phones where they can listen to the tapes. Such items greatly enlarge the teaching available in the church. Money provides good instruments to sing to. The church should be a centre. It should not have hard benches where we sit uncomfortably for an hour on Sunday morning, and another hour in the evening if we can endure it.

Money can, of course, do other things besides making Sunday a day which honours God. Some churches give a tenth of their income to foreign missions. Churches can join together to help rehabilitate alcoholics and those addicted to other drugs.

Teaching the children

Perhaps the most important activity, apart from the services, is the Sunday school. Because religious education in schools has almost ceased, Sunday school is far more important than ever it was. If we are not to be a pagan country once more, we must get the children back to Sunday school.

When our own Sunday school went into decline, we told ourselves that this was inevitable. The days of Sunday school for the tough urban child were over. But one middle-aged lady in our church was conscience stricken. She agitated until we bought a mini-bus to tour round the local council estates to collect children. Our young people knocked on doors and volunteered to teach. At last we had a Sunday school once more.

Trial and error showed us who could handle these tough kids, who could grip their attention, who could persuade the boys that Sunday school was not for girls and under-tens. It is a continual fight to keep the children, and there are hard and disappointing times. But gradually a personal relationship has been built up. The children's personal identities emerge from the gang. They begin to find a place in the church – even if Sunday tea is now more rowdy than it was. Nobody wanted to teach at first – especially the professional school-teachers, who were at it all week. But now that the children are there, nobody can refuse. Taking a class every Sunday is a tough discipline, but well worth while. It can be one of the most encouraging and worthwhile of activities.

Sunday is meant to be used positively. It is no good our laying down a series of strict rules, as the Pharisees did, about what is forbidden on the sabbath. If we fill the day with useful activity, we will have no need of rules. Otherwise we will find that the rules are useless because they are either resented or not kept.

Young children are part of the church. We cannot treat them as 'mere pagans'. But while children can stand one service – or part of a service – and Sunday school, we cannot expect them to appreciate Sunday as the adult Christian can. It seems best, with children, to treat Sunday as a special day. It is a day when parents do things with them that they would not normally do on a busy weekday – a day when dad and mum are both available, to tell stories, to listen, to talk and do other things which are not done on weekdays. It should not be a day when mum and dad sleep all afternoon, and nobody must make a sound.

A challenge to assumptions

Sunday is the day when the Christian and the non-Christian must obviously go their separate ways. For six days there may be little outward difference, but on the seventh there is. The non-Christian does not want to remember God and the Christian does. The non-Christian wants to take all the benefits; food, health, life, family. But he does not want to owe God anything. Sunday is the day when those assumptions are challenged by the minority who go in public to thank God for his gifts, to praise him for his blessings and to pray for his mercy.

The seventh day was set aside as a special day from the beginning of time. It reminds man of his Creator. It reminds us of the work of creation. It preserves a knowledge of God the Creator. It reminds us that the physical world in which we live did not come first. Behind it there is a spiritual world, of which we are also part. It is day free for teaching about God, and worship of God. On the first day of the week, it commemorates the rising of Christ from the dead. The sign from God to the world that all that he taught was true.

Chapter 5
Parents and children

Honour your father and your mother, that your days
be long in the land which the Lord your God gives you.

The apostle Paul points out that this is the first commandment
with a promise, so there is a special blessing from it. If we
honour our parents, society will be strengthened, and its life
prolonged. It is obvious, if you think about it. If accumulated
wisdom can be passed on, we are less likely to make disastrous
mistakes of the sort which can bring a society down. If we
insist that there is no wisdom except what we learn ourselves,
we are far more likely to run into trouble.

This commandment is entirely against the spirit of our own
age. It contradicts about half-a-dozen of its most precious
beliefs. It is, to begin with, paternalistic. Our age does not like
the idea that wisdom can be handed down from a father-
figure. Then the commandment is against the cult of youth,
the belief that tomorrow is more important than today, and
that yesterday is completely played out. It is against the
tendency to lower the age at which the young can make up
their own mind, the age of consent, the age of majority, the age
at which protection is removed from them.

But perhaps most of all, our age opposes the idea of
obligation to the family. The fifth commandment is against
the cult of individualism, the belief that we live to ourselves
and die to ourselves; the belief that no other living soul has a
right over us to advise, to command honour or respect.

Paul spells out the command more explicitly. He says
'Children, obey your parents in the Lord, for this is right.' If
parents tell children to do something which is patently wrong
and against God's law, then the children must not do it. The
authority of the parent comes from God. It cannot be exercised
against God. But it is that authority and discipline at the heart

of society, in the family, which holds society together. The family is the smallest, most cohesive, social unit. God put it there.

Pressures on the family

Today's intellectuals seem intent on blowing the family apart. The permissive society opposes discipline, and especially discipline within the family. Moral sanctions in the family used to be backed by economic sanctions. The family was dependent on the wage-earner, and the wage-earner was normally the father. But today an unskilled sixteen-year-old can earn almost as much as his father. Since he does not have his father's obligations, the youngster's disposable income is much greater.

The young today have an economic freedom never known before – so long as they earn instead of studying. But even those who go to technical college or university do not have to depend on their parents. In Britain they are provided for by the state. If they are out of work, the state provides – it even provides for students unable to get a holiday job.

A great deal of this is a change for the better. It is good that the young can earn a decent wage. It is good that a parent's lack of income no longer prevents a son or daughter from getting the education his or her talents deserve. And the apostle Paul condemns the wilful parent as much as the disobedient child. Nor should any Christian parent have to rely mainly on economic sanctions. But both the economics of the market and of state intervention have changed the relationship. Neither change seems to have been made with much thought for the effect on the family.

Too many of today's intellectuals regard the family as a fairly low priority. Many believe it is completely unnecessary. So the advertisers can go for the enormous youth market with little restraint. The young couple may find it hard to get a house, the penniless may find it difficult to keep up with price increases. But the youth market has exploded. The advertisers flatter the young, exploit their independence, and persuade them to spend their money as fast as they can.

One advertisement shows a sports-car driven by a boy who is taking out his girl-friend. It reads: 'Some day you'll settle down with a nice, sensible girl, a nice sensible house and a nice, sensible family saloon. Some day. Meantime, let your hair down, put your hood down and push your foot down. After all, you've no commitments to slow you up. Meantime, feel the sun on your face and the wind whistling past your ears. Play tunes on the gearbox through the country back roads. True there are only two seats. Who needs a charabanc for what you have in mind?'

The growth of juvenile crime

Money and independence do not, however, solve all our problems. It used to be thought they would. With good sense we could have done better. But with the rise of youthful affluence has come a rise in youthful crime. The tidal wave of juvenile crime covers the country. The police are incapable of dealing with this breakdown of family discipline, as are the schools, and the institutions for juvenile criminals. The state is not capable of taking over the function of the family.

I have been trustee for a number of years of a youth club in South London. The warden keeps the confidence of a number of teenage gangsters. Most of them came from broken homes, transferred their loyalty to the gang, and were from time to time in trouble with the police. Faced with the rise in juvenile crime, the police are in no position to be parent-substitutes. Faced with gang loyalty, they feel themselves forced to be rough-and-ready in their methods. The warden has had particular difficulties in protecting those who really were trying to go straight, but could not convince the police.

The chief constable of a great northern city has told me that he and his men simply cannot undertake family discipline. Fathers and mothers have two or three children to look after. Each policeman has thousands. The social services are just as hard-pressed. The law works only where the vast majority are law-abiding. When the family breaks down, and thousands of youngsters go on the rampage, the ordinary process of law cannot substitute.

It is a short step from criminal youth to armed youth. It is well-known that the para-military organizations in Northern Ireland depend on teenage gunmen and bombers. Older men keep in the background, and send children out to kill and be killed. Once the authority of the parents has been destroyed, the way is open for anybody to step in.

Of course criminals and the para-military are only a fraction of the population. But the criminal statistics show a trend. There is an increase in youthful folly, and in youthful self-centredness. Young people are exercising power without responsibility, the thoughtless and careless destroying of the happiness of other people.

An idealism still remains in youth despite everything. It will be a sorry day when we no longer find young people who go against the trend, and who have a genuine and idealistic desire to make a better world. But this idealism is not produced by the breakdown of the family. All the statistics link crime and delinquency very strongly to the breakdown of the family. The family is an institution ordained by God. Even in the most adverse economic and intellectual climate, it does not break easily.

The discipline of love

This breakdown of family discipline makes it urgent and necessary for Christian families to show by example how the family should hold together. An ounce of example is worth a pound of theory. Example shows what can be done. Example cannot be denied. Its influence is far wider than any of us imagine.

But we do not behave as God tells us merely to set an example. We do it because it is right. Keeping God's laws is the best and most wholesome way to live. It is better for children and it is better for parents.

Family discipline is reciprocal. The apostle Paul tells fathers that they should not provoke their children to anger. He says elsewhere that parents should lay up for their children, and not children for parents. Christ, as a Son, was obedient to God the Father. But God the Father showed his love to God the Son in every way.

God calls for discipline with love. Children will often put up with discipline without love, though sometimes they will rebel. But parents are to love their children. True discipline goes with a love which the child knows and recognizes. The old story of the father about to beat his son saying: 'This is going to hurt me more than it hurts you,' makes us laugh, because we do not believe it. But a son who had really experienced his father's love would know that there was a hurt to the parent – even if it was not so violent and painful.

We all know parents who are rough with children. We hear small children wailing in the supermarket, as irritable mothers cuff them and drag them around. There are even, I fear, parents who ensure their children's silence in church in ways which leave little room for love or understanding.

We meet other families where the parents obviously consider their children. On any holiday beach you can see what a difference it makes. Mothers and fathers are prepared to amuse the young, and take an interest in what they are doing. They encourage them, comfort them when they are hurt. They go with them where they might be afraid, join in games, and occasionally allow themselves to be buried in sand!

In other families there are continual squalls, because the parents regard the children as a nuisance. The children are constantly wilful and disobedient, however much the parents shout. Natural obedience goes with love. Parental indifference and youthful disobedience seem to go together. In families, as elsewhere, obedience is earned by the experience of continued care. If a child knows that the parent cares, then he will believe that a warning comes from that feeling of care. If a child experiences nothing but a parent's selfishness, then he is naturally inclined to believe that an order is given for the parent's convenience.

As children grow up, the problems change. A Danish friend once warned us: 'Small children, small problems; large children, large problems!' The relationship which has been established between parents and young children begins to come under strain as the children go to school. They run into the rebelliousness of children whose parents have not taken the time and trouble with them. The pattern of life in a Christian home is questioned, and the ways of the secular world begin to make their impact.

The child of Christian parents is not automatically a Christian. Baptism alone is not enough. So we must not think anything out of the ordinary has happened when a strong streak of rebellion appears. Children of Christian parents are in the care of the church, and are especially blessed. Paul tells the Christians at Corinth: 'The unbelieving husband is consecrated through his wife, and the unbelieving wife is consecrated through her husband. Otherwise [if they parted] your children would be unclean, but as it is they are holy.'

So within a Christian family, or a family in which one parent is a Christian, the other unbelieving parent is 'consecrated' and the children are holy. But this special position comes short of the change in desires and motivation brought by Christian commitment and the work in Christians of God's Holy Spirit.

Many a Christian parent has alienated the growing child by behaving as if Christian desires and motives were natural to them. They press and persuade the child too hard to engage in Christian activities, even persuading them, by moral black-mail, to say they are Christians.

A balance has to be struck between what a teenage son or daughter can reasonably be expected to do out of natural respect for their parents, and what they should not be expected to do if they are not Christians. While children remain in the parental home, it is reasonable that there should be give and take. Parents must tolerate a certain level of noise, a certain flow of friends. They must tolerate usage of the telephone and an increased borrowing of books, clothes, records and cameras. Youthful enthusiasms should not be damped with a heavy hand.

I remember hearing of a distinguished American Christian whose son had developed an enthusiasm for tinkering with car engines. While on a family holiday, this son came upon a prize specimen. There was just room for it in the enormous family estate car. The son desperately wanted to buy the engine with his savings, and take it with them. Most fathers would have said 'Not on your life!' This man felt that his son could have worse enthusiasms than car engines, and agreed. At every stop, the engine had to be heaved out. Every time they moved on, it had to be heaved back in. Fathers who have packed holiday cars to the brim, once out and once back, will know the forbearance involved. To do it at every stop, with a casual purchase of that size and weight, approaches sainthood. But that is how youthful loyalty is earned.

On the other side, such parents can reasonably ask their teenage children to respect a Christian home. They can ask them to come to church at least once on Sunday, to keep within the law, to respect the other sex and to guard their language. They can require them not to get into bad company, or go to wild parties, to study hard, or work hard to earn their living. A great many parents will feel they can go well beyond this, even though their children are not Christian. Many children will want to go beyond, because they genuinely respect their parents. But there is a minimum, and the Christian parent should try to insist on that minimum.

The wisdom of ages

The Bible has a great deal to say about wisdom. It is an underrated virtue. Knowledge is today's God. Science is the answer to everything. Today's science is better than yesterday's.

But without wisdom, knowledge is useless. The young may accumulate knowledge quickly. They may have more knowledge than their parents. But wisdom comes more slowly. It comes by experience, and through progressive knowledge of human nature. It comes through increasing self-discipline, which curbs the rashness of youth. The Bible has one whole book on wisdom, 'The Proverbs of Solomon':

'That men may know wisdom and instruction,
    understand words of insight,
receive instruction in wise dealing,
    righteousness, justice, and equity;
that prudence may be given to the simple,
    knowledge and discretion to the youth . . .
The fear of the Lord is the beginning of knowledge;
    fools despise wisdom and instruction.
Hear, my son, your father's instruction,
    And reject not your mother's teaching.'

And so he goes on, as a father instructing his son in wisdom. He warns against every kind of folly: bad companions, the loose woman, giving pledges to strangers, indolence – 'Go to the ant thou sluggard, consider her ways and be wise'. He warns against the smooth tongue of the adventuress and the harlot. He encourages him to respect the greatness of God, by whom kings reign, who 'brought forth the springs of water' and shaped the mountains.

The book contrasts wisdom with folly, the son who listens with the scoffer. It is full of memorable quotations, all as true today as ever they were. 'A soft answer turns away wrath, but a harsh word stirs up anger.' 'Better is a dry morsel with quiet than a house full of feasting and strife.' 'Wine is a mocker, strong drink a brawler; and whoever is led astray by it is not wise.' 'It is an honour for a man to keep aloof from strife; but every fool will be quarrelling.' 'Answer not a fool according to his folly, lest you be like him yourself. Answer a fool according to his folly, lest he be wise in his own eyes.'

The society in which we live is very different from the society of King Solomon's day. But human nature is the same. The wisdom of Solomon is as sound today as it was then. The fool, the lazy, the scoffer, the loose woman, the bad companion are all here. We may call them by different names – as one euphemism follows another to conceal evils we do not want to recognize. But the wise will see them for what they are, and the foolish will not. The proverb my own father used to repeat to me was: 'A prudent man sees danger and hides himself; but the simple go on, and suffer for it.'

There are, of course, all kinds of reasons why the young will not listen. They are bombarded by the media as never before. The teenage pop-culture is powerful. Temptations are attractive. The young are innocent of the suffering which folly brings. Sometimes it is only the hurt which stops them. Then it brings with it a bitterness which sours the sweetness of youth.

No young person likes to be far out of line with his peer-group. A group at school or in the same neighbourhood can pull each other down. So the young have to make their own mistakes. Meantime they suffer more from the unrestrained and greedy commercial exploitation of their weaknesses.

Those who exploit sex in pornographic and near-pornographic magazines, books, films and records have much to answer for. A great deal of other writing and comment is hedonistic and living-for-the-moment, or pessimistic and destructive. Too little is balanced and wise.

The rise in education has also brought quite new problems. Each generation stays longer at school. More children tend to go on to higher education. The son and daughter with 'A' levels and degrees, who grow up more affluent and sophisticated than their parents, tend to look down on parental wisdom as 'too simple'.

As technology and communications progress we tend to think that our parents and their wisdom are no more relevant than the technologies of their time. 'Never stand behind the rear-legs of a horse,' said father to son, for generation after generation. To the urban child of the motor age such advice is irrelevant. He thinks much other advice equally irrelevant.

Mothers advised their daughters to keep young men a certain distance, lest they have an unwanted pregnancy. Now, with techniques to avoid unwanted pregnancy, daughters are tempted to discount all advice. Parents urged children to work, so that they should not go hungry. Now, in our proper care for the needy and our anxiety that this care should be a right, no child will go hungry if he does not work. So that bit of wisdom also seems out-dated.

Children who cannot remember, and who do not read history, find it hard to believe that in a lifetime they may well live through different conditions. In a country which ignores the wisdom of its parents, they most certainly will. An individual may be protected by society. But where society goes wrong, there is no one to protect him. Wisdom leaves no careless gaps, but folly is soon destroyed.

That other book of wisdom, Ecclesiastes, tells us: 'Woe to you, O land, when your king is a child.' Translated for modern society, we might read: 'Woe, to you, O land, when you are led by juvenile ideas.'

Nor should we be led by modern ideologies. Every time we find wisdom met by a slogan, we should be put on our guard. Those who want to tear down shout 'Reactionist!' against those who want tried and tested wisdom to stand.

The Christian wants change. The Christian is the last person to tolerate power, privilege and oppression. He is the first to want to improve the health and wealth of the community. Christ did not tolerate the world of the Pharisees and Sadducees, and the money-changers in the temple. The economic system of slavery collapsed before the advance of Christianity. So the Christian should always be a reformer. It is those who thoughtlessly tear down, the 'rebels without a cause', who breed reaction. If they take to violence, they are met with violence.

All through the Bible we read of the respect paid by youth to age, and the trouble which follows when age and experience are ignored.

At least one of Solomon's sons did not read his father's wisdom. When Rehoboam succeeded his father Solomon we read that he 'took counsel with the old men, who had stood before Solomon his father' and they advised him to '"be a servant to this people today and serve them and speak good words to them when you answer them, then they will be your servants for ever." But he forsook the counsel which the old men gave him, and took counsel with the young men who had grown up with him.'

On their advice he answered the people harshly. This split the kingdom, dividing the strength of Israel and setting tribe against tribe. The young men took Israel's strength for granted. They had only known the power and glory of Solomon's kingdom. They had not remembered the divisions of David's day and the desperate struggles against the Philistines. They wanted to maintain and increase the taxes which supported Solomon's glory.

The old men remembered that power was based on a united Israel and on the consent of the people. They remembered that the monarchy was new. Rehoboam was only the fourth king. They were not dazzled by modern trends, they took nothing for granted. They knew the structure of power, how precariously it was built, and how easily it could fall. Civilization had not lulled them. They were anxious and alert. It was the young men who were complacent and obtuse. Their wits had not yet been sharpened by life.

There are, of course, limits to the wisdom of age. Parents can abuse their position. In the East it is still the custom to arrange marriages. Christians have to resist the tendency of parents to marry a daughter, for instance, to a boy whose Christianity is only skin-deep. Many non-Christian parents are shocked by the new life led by children who have become Christians. They try to justify their own way of life by pressing their children to follow. But Christians do not have to follow because, as Paul says, obedience is to be 'in the Lord'.

But the Christian must still honour the non-Christian father and mother. The Old Testament commandment had no qualification to the command to 'honour'. All parents are entitled to respect. This is often one of the most difficult commands for new converts. They find that their parents are wrong about the thing that matters most. They proceed to lecture them about it, and disregard them in everything else. Such an attitude makes few converts among parents.

But no parent can fail to be impressed when a child who has just become a Christian begins to treat them with a new respect, to listen to them, to consider their wishes, to be helpful around the house, doing chores which had always been neglected. That kind of respect can bring new converts. Respect for parents never ceases. Joseph respected his father Jacob when he was an old man, and so we should always honour our parents.

But a change comes at marriage. As Jesus said, 'He who made them from the beginning made them male and female, and said, "For this reason a man shall leave his father and mother and be joined to his wife, and the two shall become one.'" There is a new relationship and a new loyalty which everybody, including parents, must respect.

Limits to match-making

It is at the point just before marriage that a final crisis sometimes comes. A son or a daughter wants to marry somebody of whom the parents do not approve. The 'new romanticism' sees no problem. Everybody has to live to himself, and parents should be disregarded. Love must triumph. This has been the theme of thousands of romantic novels.

Yet this is not how most of the world has lived. Marriages have been arranged since Abraham sent his servant to find a wife for Isaac. Love came on marriage – Isaac 'took Rebekah and she became his wife and he loved her'.

Which is right, the arranged marriage or romantic love? In Japan, which now has both systems, opinion seems to be that neither shows a clear advantage or disadvantage over the other. Both produce happy and unhappy marriages. There is no doubt that parents, motivated by social snobbery, pride or greed can subordinate the true happiness of the couple.

Dynastic marriages are not naturally happy. Yet pity the poor little rich girl. How is she to know that a man is not marrying her for money, unless he has as much as she has? Pity the poor prince, who can make his wife a queen, or the lord, who can make his wife a lady. How do they know they are truly loved, and not the object of ambition? Mary Queen of Scots married beneath her. Her husband turned out to be an ambitious fool. Her cousin, Queen Elizabeth, decided it was safer to be the Virgin Queen.

Marriage for love ought to be happy. Yet many people, when they think of life as it might have been with their first teenage sweetheart, recoil in horror at the very idea. They are happy that some sixth sense, some friend or a parent gave a kindly hint. The divorce rates decline as the age at marriage rises. Teenage marriages produce the highest rate of divorce.

But parents should be beware of speaking out. It is not easy to tell who will suit whom. After twenty years' teaching a class of young people, including one year when sixteen of them married among themselves, I am still unable to predict who will match with whom. A flamboyant character will sometimes marry a quiet girl who will keep him in order with little difficulty. And yet sometimes two strong characters can marry, and the sparks do not fly as might be expected. In the end, after a great deal of too-ing and fro-ing, it seems to sort itself out. To interfere is seldom wise or right.

Although it is best to allow these matters to sort themselves out, parents do owe children a duty. A marriage will have to sustain a family. Parents have the duty to point out that two do not live as cheaply as one, and three certainly do not. It does not help the early days of marriage to live in poverty while studying for exams.

Within a church community of those who have known each other, parents and children, over the years, matches may sort out fairly easily. But parents should point out the problems of marriage between those of different nations and races. Unspoken – and therefore unknown – assumptions may be entirely different.

Yet even here, there are exceptions. I once spoke to a very distinguished audience of the problems of Europeans marrying American wives. This was only to discover that my hostess, whose husband had been British Ambassador to the USA, was herself an American. She did not let me forget it. An elderly lawyer in Ireland once received a telegram from his son, 'Am coming home with a wife.' She turned out to be Japanese. When her husband, an RAF pilot, was killed, she stayed on to look after the old man.

Yet mixed marriages have very real and understandable problems. Some relationships can end tragically before marriage. Late one afternoon we received a phone call from a young African student. His fiancée had committed suicide. He had ignored African custom by choosing his own bride. His fiancée, a British girl, was autistic, while the African was a cheerful extrovert. She must have felt overwhelmed by him, and unable to express her problem. In despair she ended her life. He blamed his ignoring of parental advice for the tragedy. Later he happily married a girl of like background, approved by his parents, able to keep on his level.

Given trust, forbearance, and a real and obvious love of parent for child, the relationship between parents and children can survive different views on prospective husbands and wives. But it is good when all the family, with their continuous close relations, can really welcome a new son or new daughter, and love them as if they were their own.

Chapter 6
Concern for life

You shall not kill.

When we come to the sixth commandment, most of us probably have some feeling of relief. Here, at last, is a command of which we are not guilty. The number of murders may be growing, but it is fortunately still very small. It is unlikely to include any of us.

But that was not how Christ saw the sixth commandment. In the Sermon on the Mount he said 'You have heard that it was said to the men of old "You shall not kill; and whoever kills shall be liable to judgment." But I say to you that everyone who is angry with his brother shall be liable to judgment; whoever insults his brother shall be liable to the council, and whoever says, "You fool!" shall be liable to the hell of fire.' Christ sharpens the edge of every commandment. He goes to the heart, and shows the evil there that leads to the sin. He wants us to resist the sin at the beginning. The beginning of the outward act of murder is the sin of anger and hatred. The very first murder, of Abel by Cain, arose from jealous anger.

The difference in law between anger and murder is that the first is inward and cannot be proved in a court of law to have harmed anybody, while the latter is an outward act which can be proved. But Our Lord is saying that, in God's sight, the anger is just as much an offence. It is just as deserving of judgement.

Racial hatred
The most destructive hatred of the twentieth century has been racialism. It has led to war, and the mass murder of innocent men, women and children. Twenty million Russians lost their lives in the World War II as did six million Jews. The figures

are so high that we find them difficult to take in. Yet racialism can start so innocently. It appeals to our sense of loyalty to all we know and love – our own people, our country, our history, our flag, and all the other symbols which seem threatened by strangers.

It is too easy to identify the Christian church with our own country; to forget that it is worldwide, that God is the God of all mankind; and to forget that Christ told the Jews the parable of the good Samaritan to teach them that they should love their Samaritan neighbours, and not despise them.

For nationalist movements, such as the Jewish nationalist movement of Christ's time, can easily be divisive and breed hate, which soon breeds violence and death. They set the Basque againt the Spaniard; the Breton against the Frenchman; the Quebecois against the Canadian; the Croat against the Serb; the Catalan against the Castilian; the Ibo against the Yoruiba; the German against the Jew and the Slav; the Flamand against the Walloon; the Irish against the Ulsterman; the Scots, Irish and Welsh against the English; and the English against the Pakistani and West Indian. There is no end to it, so it is better that there should be no beginning. We should learn to love our neighbour and our brother instead of hating him.

Love forgives all things
The answer to hatred is love. It is not enough to put our brother out of our mind. We must be reconciled to him. This is not a position of armed neutrality. It is positive. We must be on good terms. We cannot worship God while we are on bad terms with our brother. As the apostle John says, 'If a person does not love the brother whom he has seen, how can he love God, whom he has not seen.'

We must not allow grievances to linger on. They should be settled at once. So let us settle grievances between fellow Christians urgently, lest we have to answer while there is bitterness still in our hearts.

There is nothing that brings a church into bad repute as much as the continued quarrels of its members, people or groups not speaking to each other. Yet it happens all too often. Few of us have not known churches like that. But, we say, what if the fault is on the other side? It is surely up to the person who is in the wrong to put it right. When Peter asked, '"Lord, how often shall my brother sin against me, and I forgive him? As many as seven times?" Jesus said to him, "I do not say to you seven times, but seventy times seven.""

It is inconceivable to most people that forgiveness should be one-sided. Yet that is the Christian rule. We imagine that everybody would take advantage of those who are so forgiving. But our knowledge of human nature is not as great as God's. The spirit of genuine forgiveness is a state of mind, not a matter of calculation. We must always forgive.

In the prayer the Lord himself taught us, he tells us to pray that God will 'Forgive us our debts, as we also have forgiven our debtors.' It is clear that we cannot expect forgiveness from God unless we too forgive. It is conditional. We have to have faith to be forgiven, we *also* have to have the spirit of forgiveness in us. Both are from God; both come together. How can we expect God to forgive us if we will not, in our turn, forgive our brother?

We all find forgiveness hard. For example, a couple have been engaged for two years. Then one of them decides it is all over. It is hard for the other to forgive. We trust somebody and they let us down. We work for a hard and ungrateful boss, who sacks us to further his own interests. It is difficult not to be bitter. Somebody marries our daughter, then walks out and leaves her with a child to care for. Somebody poisons the mind of a friend against us.

Christ knows all this. His own friend, Judas, betrayed him to the enemies who wanted his life. His disciples deserted him. Peter denied that he ever knew him. Yet Christ forgave Peter. Peter, in turn, later gave his life for Christ.

Another powerful illustration is David's loyalty to King Saul, who, through jealousy, hounded him for his life. David protected himself, warned by Saul's son Jonathan. But twice, when Saul's life was in David's hands, he let him go. His spirit was never bitter, always forgiving. He did his best, after Saul's death, to reconcile Saul's remaining family.

We cannot protect ourselves, as we think, by our continued bitterness. If we do what is right, then God will protect us, and that is far more secure. But we find, so often, that a forgiving spirit produces the right response. Any bitterness on the other side is thawed by a spirit of forgiveness. It takes two to keep a difference alive. If we ignore it determinedly, then it is hard for anybody else to keep it up. Smiles and friendliness do not always produce warmth, but often they do. So we should try, and see what happens.

Otherwise quarrels tend to be self-perpetuating. They take on a life of their own, until nobody can remember what the first cause was. As insults are exchanged, a small cloud can gather into a great storm. The only way out is forgiveness. No personal quarrel is ever going to be settled in any other way.

Is violence justifiable?

The failure to forgive leads us from the quarrel to the feud, and from insults to violence. Of course nobody intends that it should end in violence. But in an atmosphere of hatred, weak and unbalanced minds begin to conceive evil deeds. Words are not enough, something must be done.

Violence does not occur in a vacuum. It needs an atmosphere of hostility. We worry about black neighbours. We wish they were not there. We begin to talk about it. Older people talk, and the young listen. Soon there is an atmosphere of distrust and hostility. In this atmosphere the first violence takes place.

Was President Kennedy's assassination a plot? Did Lee Harvey Oswald act on his own? We may never know the truth. But we do know that many were hostile to the President. Many wished him dead. This created an atmosphere of hostility in which the seed of violence could be sown. It grew in the mind until it blossomed into a sinister deed. So hatred in the mind turns to a deed of hate.

But are not some violent deeds justified? To assassinate a democratically-elected president is terrible. But would it have been so terrible to kill a tyrant, such as Hitler? There are tyrants today with murder on their hands. Some church leaders ask for their overthrow – though without saying how.

The feeling today is that assassination is justified for political ends. Both nationalism and Marxism are totalitarian creeds. They teach that nothing will really be right until their party comes to power. Everything turns on the political system. Anybody who stands in the way of political change stands in the way of the people's good. The end justifies the means. Assassination is a pity, but if there is no other way to change the system, what are the people to do? So even churches collect money which finds its way to pay for arms for 'freedom-fighters'.

The Christian takes a more sceptical view of political change. The Psalmist tells us 'Put not your trust in princes.' We believe that all men are sinners – the Marxists as well as the conservatives, the nationalists as well as the imperialists. As sinners, they are open to corruption. The despotism of the Bourbon monarchs gives way, after the French Revolution, to the despotism of Napoleon. As the French say, 'The more it changes the more it is the same thing.' The despotism of the Czar gives way, after the Russian Revolution, to the despotism of Stalin. The Kaiser gives way to Hitler. Even Cromwell could not keep the power he gained by force without the continued use of force. After his death the monarchy was restored.

The teaching of Christ, of Paul and of Peter is that we must respect civil government. It is ordained of God. Christ taught that we should 'Render to Caesar the things that are Caesar's and to God the things that are God's.' Paul wrote: 'Let every person be subject to the governing authorities. For there is no authority except from God.' Peter wrote: 'Be subject for the Lord's sake to every human institution, whether it be to the emperor as supreme, or to governors as sent by him to punish those who do wrong and to praise those who do right.' Christ told those who drew swords to defend him on his arrest to sheath their swords for 'All who take the sword will perish by the sword.'

Nobody reading these passages can doubt their meaning. And Christ and the two apostles were talking not of a democratically-elected national government practising religious toleration, but of a militarist, persecuting, imperialist government. So there do not seem to be obvious justifications for Christians to advocate tyrannicide. That is not the Christian way of changing the world.

Christ told Pilate, 'My kingship is not of this world; if my kingship were of this world, my servants would fight, that I might not be handed over to the Jews; but my kingship is not from the world.' Christianity has not spread by the sword of steel but by changing men's minds. Not by political power, but by the power of example. Of course politically-powerful men have tried to use the faith for their own ends. But a profession of faith imposed by the sword does not last when the sword has gone.

The defence of the realm

At the other extreme are the pacifists. They claim that not even the state is entitled to use the sword. They believe that the state should turn the other cheek, as Christ told his disciples to do in the Sermon on the Mount. But this is to confuse the state with the individual. We are not, as individuals, to take the law into our own hands. Paul tells us 'Repay no one evil for evil . . . for it is written "Vengeance is mine, I will repay" says the Lord.' But as we have seen, God has instituted the state as the ordinary means of doing this.

God will punish the wicked at the final judgement even if they escape the state. But Paul says that, meantime: 'If you do wrong, be afraid, for [the governing authority] does not bear the sword in vain; he is the servant of God to execute his wrath on the wrongdoer.' So governments are there to bear the sword to protect every citizen. If they do not do this, they neglect their God-ordained duty.

The pacifist may still argue that, though internal security may be a duty of government, Christians should not fight in wars against other countries. But the principle remains the same. The state has the duty to protect the citizen against his enemies, whether they are internal or external.

It is not easy today to draw the line. Violence against the citizen is violence, whether it comes from a gang of criminals or a gang which purports to be fighting on behalf of an international political cause. Nor is it really practical to ask the majority of citizens in the majority of countries to decide for themselves whether a war is a just war, whether it is a war of defence or a war of aggression.

In democracies, citizens are informed by a free press and Christians can throw their political influence on the side of peace. Even there they can be wrong. For example the democracies were almost certainly wrong to appease Hitler in the 1930s. But how can the citizen in a dictatorship, with a controlled press and little access to impartial information, know whether his country is being threatened, or is itself the cause of tension? We should not be too hard on the soldier who is called to defend his country. When the repentant soldiers asked John the Baptist what to do, he told them not to abuse their power. He did not tell them to go back home. Christ did not tell the centurion of great faith to give up his sword; nor did Peter tell Cornelius, the centurion whom he converted in

Caesarea, to leave the army.

There is abuse of military power today as there was then. After the World War II soldiers on the losing side who abused their power were rightly brought to trial. But it is also an abuse of power to use weapons of mass-destruction, which kill soldier and civilian indiscriminately. Christians are right to press for the banning of these weapons, and to argue against the concept of 'total war'. But Our Lord said there will be 'wars and rumours of wars' until the end of time. A Christian cannot argue that pacifism will abolish war.

The necessity of capital punishment

There is another kind of pacifism today. This is the denial to the state of its duty to bear the sword against murderers. In the last twenty-five years, in the countries where the laws have been based on the Christian ethic, the penalty of capital punishment for murder has been abolished under humanist pressure. It is, of course, understandable that humanists, who do not believe in life after death, should feel compelled to preserve even the life of a murderer.

But crimes of violence and murder have risen dramatically. It is a fair assumption that the dramatic increase in murder and violence are both connected with the abolition of capital punishment. It is the major and most dramatic change in penal law. Almost all the other factors which affect crimes of violence were the same twenty-five years ago as they are today. Crimes such as kidnapping for ransom are much more common. Piracy has returned in its modern form of hijacking aircraft, and holding passengers' lives to ransom. This deterioration in the rule of law is common to all the countries where capital punishment has been abolished. It does not seem to be found in Marxist countries, or in other countries which retain the death penalty.

Many leaders in the Christian church accept the humanist view. Yet surely the Christian's task is to question conventional wisdom. The Christian should put it alongside Christian doctrine, and compare the two with the utmost rigour. The Christian church has held one view for almost 2,000 years, and its Jewish predecessors for about 1,000 years before that. Surely the traditional Christian view should be debated, and not ignored by church leaders. The new view should not be allowed to capture the Christian church without at least a token argument.

It is therefore necessary to look at the Christian view again. It has been held so positively, unambiguously and certainly throughout the centuries that it is, in some ways, odd to have to restate it. It is perhaps best put in the words of four respected commentators on the passage in Genesis where God promised: 'I will never again curse the ground because of man, for the imagination of man's heart is evil from his youth; neither will I ever again destroy every living creature as I have done. While the earth remains, seedtime and harvest, summer and winter, cold and heat, day and night, shall not cease.' God has kept his word. Even our measurement of time past depends on our belief in stability of natural laws, for we cannot measure time past except on that assumption.

There are only two conditions to this covenant. One is that we should not eat animal flesh full of blood, for blood symbolizes life, which we must respect. The other condition is, 'For your lifeblood I will surely require a reckoning; of every beast I will require it and of man. Whoever sheds the blood of man, by man shall his blood be shed; for God made man in his own image.'

All four commentators interpret this as a covenant for all time. It teaches that capital punishment for murder is obligatory.

In 1554, the reformer John Calvin said, 'God so threatens vengeance against the murderer that he even arms the magistrate with the sword for avenging of slaughter in order that the blood of men may not be shed with impunity. Since [men] bear the image of God upon them, he deems himself violated in their person. No one can be injurious to his brother without wounding God himself.'

In 1683, Matthew Poole said, 'The magistrate is hereby empowered and required upon pain of God's highest displeasure to inflict this punishment. Murder is not only an offence against man, but also an injury to God and a contempt of that image of God which all men are obliged to reverence and maintain, especially magistrates, who being God's vice-regents and servants are therefore under a particular obligation to punish those who deface and destroy it.'

In 1706, Matthew Henry said, 'Wilful murder must always be punished with death. It is a sin which the Lord would not pardon in a prince . . . and which a prince therefore should not pardon in a subject. Such remains of God's image are still upon fallen man as that he who unjustly kills a man, defaces the image of God and does dishonour to him.'

In 1898, Bishop Ellicott wrote, 'The penalty of life for life is not to be left to natural law, but man himself, in such a manner and with such safeguards as the civil law in each country shall order, is to execute the divine command.'

Many today argue that the Old Testament is no longer binding. It is true that the civil penalties in the Jewish Law are not binding. Christ forgave the woman taken in adultery. It was still a sin and needed forgiveness. But the penalty laid down in the time of Moses had clearly fallen into disuse. When challenged to restore it, Jesus did not do so. But the covenant between God and man in Genesis chapter eight is not part of a changing civil code, which can be altered to take account of the times. It is part of the moral law, and it cannot be abolished. We still live under the covenant under which God preserves the world against universal catastrophe, and maintains the stability of its natural laws. The commands which went with the covenant still hold.

Some people also argue that if we are going to rely on the Old Testament, we should go right back to the first murderer, Cain. Not only did God not take Cain's life, but he actually protected him from the vengeance of others. So, from the very beginning, it is argued, God showed mercy. But that is not the end of the story. Cain himself did not perish by a violent death. But the civilization which he fathered perished it its entirety. Cain's offspring became so corrupt, and so corrupted others, that God had to start again with one family from the line of Cain's younger brother, Seth. To ensure that there will be no similar universal catastrophe in our own age, we are told that we are not to allow murder to corrupt it. The covenant with the founder of our own age supercedes the dealing of God with man in the age of Cain and his descendants. If we are to take the Old Testament as Christ and the apostles took it, there can be no doubt of its messsage.

Today's church leaders who defend the abolition of capital punishment do not do so on Christian grounds. They argue on political grounds, where they have no more competence than the rest of us. In a letter to *The Times* on 10 December 1975, a group of senior churchmen condemned terrorism as absolutely incompatible with the Christian faith. But they said that the introduction of capital punishment would be a victory for the terrorists. It would equate Britain with tyrannical governments.

This is a wholly political judgement, based on the appearance Britain would present to other governments and peoples. It ignores the fact that until recently all democracies imposed capital punishment for any kind of murder. Their second argument is that capital punishment would create martyrs – which it might – and bring civil war nearer. This is another political judgement, and no more likely to be right than the first. They argue that it would impose an appalling responsibility on the Home Secretary. They seem to ignore the appalling responsibility imposed on governments when terrorists take innocent hostages.

Then they argue, as Christians, that judgement on life and death must be left to God. But a government cannot take this attitude if terrorists hold hostages. There are times when governments, the ultimate power in the country, have to decide who lives and who dies. They try to see – so far as they can – that the innocent live, rather than the guilty.

But the quotation the writers give 'Vengeance is mine, says the Lord, I will repay' is taken from Paul's letter to the Romans. It is addressed to the individual Christians in Rome, telling them not to take the law into their own hands. 'If your enemy is hungry, feed him; if he is thirsty give him something to drink'. Paul also tells them that the ruler 'does not bear the sword for nothing. He is God's servant, an agent of justice to bring punishment on the wrong doer.'

The letter-writers end by arguing 'Our will to build a compassionate society leads us to the conviction that justice is not best served by retribution. The sanctity of human life is indivisible.' The Christian Bible argues, on the contrary, that reverence for the sanctity of human life demands that no murderer shall live.

I was once kept waiting rather a long time when I called to see Anthony Barber, while he was Chancellor of the Exchequer. He was most apologetic. He had been kept on the telephone by an old Royal Air Force friend, who had an idea on how the government could extricate the passengers of three planes held by Palestinian guerillas on a disused airfield in Jordan. He said, 'We were POWs together, and he was the tail-end-Charlie on all the escape tunnels. You can't cut off an old friend like that when he's trying to help.'

Since then many people have been trying to help all kinds of governments to deal with the problem of hostages. Jordan dealt with it by driving the guerillas out of their country into the weaker, and more divided, country of Lebanon. The Dutch government rescued a whole train from a South Moluccan group. The Irish government rescued a Dutch businessman, and the British government rescued a couple held hostage in their Marylebone flat. Most spectacular of all, the Israelis rescued a plane-load from Entebbe.

But gradually governments have hardened their line. They are no longer prepared to make concessions to killers. Herr Schleyer, the leading German industrialist, lost his life. Signor Moro, the former Italian Prime Minister, was also killed.

The problem is that the balance of threats is unequal. The killers can threaten to kill their hostages – and there is no reason to suppose that they will not kill. But a government cannot threaten to kill them if they do this. There is no credible deterrent. Then when the killers are in prison, their friends take hostages whom they threaten to kill unless they are released. As governments become more reluctant to do this, people such as Schleyer and Moro have to die; the innocent in the place of the guilty.

Those of us who go regularly to Northern Ireland have had to consider what we would want if we were taken hostage. Our own lives, or freedom for killers in prison to come out to kill more innocents? Such thoughts certainly concentrate the mind on the problem.

The police also have a problem when pursuing the ordinary criminal. Such men are now tempted to kill any witness who can identify them, since the punishment for murder is only slightly greater than the punishment for other serious crimes. And since the difference between the crime of murder and other crimes of violence is only one of degree, there is not the restraint on violence that there once was.

The figures speak for themselves. Murder has risen four and a half times in twenty-five years; crimes of violence by nine times. That needs some explaining. No satisfactory explanation has been made. It is said that there is no evidence that the reintroduction of capital punishment would lower the rate. But it is hard to know what evidence would convince.

There are other causes for increased violence, such as the break-up of the family. But there were also arguments that more education, higher incomes and social security would reduce the crime rate. But the gradual phasing out of capital punishment, and its eventual abolition, have coincided with this unprecedented rise in crimes of violence. The Christian is left with little reason to doubt the validity of the Christian rule that governments must not allow murderers to live.

Suicide is not an option

It has been the traditional Christian view that prohibition of murder also prohibits suicide. God has given us life. God alone is entitled to take our life away. Once suicide becomes a valid possibility, it can prey on the depressed mind. We are no more entitled to take our own life than we are entitled to take the life of another.

God has put us here for a purpose. We are to fulfil that purpose until he himself allows us to leave. We are not here for ourselves. We do not live to ourselves or die to ourselves. Who knows what God has for us to do, even though we are weak and helpless. We are not entitled to ask doctors or relatives to take our lives. Nobody is entitled to make another the instrument of his suicide.

Today we have the means to care for those who are fatally ill. There are hospices which make a speciality of this. They do great good, enabling the dying to live their last months with little pain, and doing a great deal to offset the distressing symptoms of the illness. They make the patient feel that he is wanted and cared for, and that all his days, including the last ones, are significant.

The work of the Samaritans too is a great help in bringing the depressed through a suicidal patch, and giving them the will to live. There are people who owe their lives to friends who have taken time and patience in those terrible periods. It is a work well worth doing. A society which makes suicide a respectable option does not help those who are tempted at such times.

Sometimes there is an element of cowardice in suicide. People are sometimes not prepared to face the consequences of their actions, and leave their problems to others. Or they are not prepared to face society, stripped of their own pretensions. They leave behind husbands, wives, sons and daughters, who have to live with the horror, and readjust their lives as best they can.

The pros and cons of abortion

Some people would also put abortion into the category of murder. The Bible says nothing about abortion. But a mother is given an instinct to protect her unborn child. It was considered a particularly horrible crime for enemies to rip up a woman with child.

Children were regarded as a gift from God. A barren womb was a personal tragedy. It is rare for an action to be unmentionable in the Bible, which mentions most of the unmentionable sins. Maybe abortion was not merely unmentionable, but unthinkable.

Yet it is not clear that abortion comes into the category of murder. An unborn child is not yet 'man made in the image of God', a thinking rational being. Maybe a newborn baby is not quite in the image of God, but there is a continuity from it of a separate independent being, who very quickly makes its personality felt. The law has always distinguished infanticide from abortion, and infant death from miscarriage.

It is surely the purpose of abortion which must be questioned. Most Christians have felt it is justified to save the life of the mother. Maybe we have stretched the point to protect the health of a sickly mother with heavy family commitments. There are Christians who believe abortion could be justified if doctors could diagnose a foetus which has a chronic malfunction. But most Christians feel that abortion solely for the convenience of the mother – because she is unmarried or does not want a child – is wrong. This goes against the natural instinct which God gave to mothers, and only harm can come from it.

Even the former pro-abortionists have been horrified as the number of abortions has risen to one for every four live-births. They do not see, nor can the average person, that such a number of abortions can be justified by the conditions laid down in the law. The medical services are also appalled at the enormous diversion of medical effort – from those who are sick to deal with nearly a hundred thousand healthy and careless women a year. It is not enough to say in reply that the children are 'unwanted', and must be destroyed in case their mothers treat them like dirt. They should not be destroyed, and their mothers should care for them – as indeed should their fathers.

We have sunk low as a society if we can no longer depend on a mother's instinctive love for her child – whatever she may have thought before it was born. And if she does not love it, there is a good chance that a foster-mother can be found who will take her place.

Caring for other people

Few of us are tempted to the crime of murder. But most of us could do a great deal more than we do to respect and preserve human life. If we are horrified by violence, I wonder whether we should ever allow it to become part of our entertainment. For today violence has become part of the entertainment industry, in films, TV, books and comics. It is not easy to prove a close connection between violence on the screen and violent crime. But can anybody who believes that violence to man, made in God's image, is violence to God himself, find violence entertaining? It is reasonable to believe that constant exposure to violence on the screen and in books is likely to deaden our instincts, so that we are less shocked by violence in real life.

The Christian should also do what he can to keep young people out of mischief. He should help provide clubs, and give time and energy, making for a sense of belonging somewhere, which those with broken homes need especially.

Each age has some folly which it takes for granted, but which looks incredible to ages following. Future ages will find today's toll of death and injury on the road an incredible folly. As Christians, we should each do our best to keep it down. There are Christians who regard bad driving as an amusing eccentricity.

There is too little between the driving of those who hold Christian standards of care for others and those who do not. But nobody who loves his brother as himself should drive carelessly, risking the lives of others. Nobody who has worked in a hospital casualty department regards careless driving as an amusing eccentricity. Despite its number-plates, a car is anonymous and enclosed, cut off from more human contact. Unless we take care, we can lose our human touch and care as soon as we get behind the wheel.

No Christian can guarantee, by safe and careful driving, that he will not injure anybody. We all have moments when we are less alert than we should be. But no Christian should, by his rashness or carelessness, be responsible for the blinding, crippling, suffering or death of another human being. Let us have Christ's love in us at all times and in every place.

Christians might also show their care for human life by taking an interest in safety at work. There must be many factories where volunteers would be welcome on the safety committee or as safety officers. For all the safety systems rely on people who care to make sure that they will work. Those of us who have to read accident reports are amazed at the ingenuity which people use to cut out safety-devices, and put their lives at risk.

I remember one fatal accident on a machine which stopped automatically when the operator stepped off it. The safety-guards could only be opened by the operation of a switch well away from the machine. The man who was killed had made a long pole, by which he could reach the safety-guard switch without stepping off the machine. On construction sites with temporary overhead power-lines, there are strict regulations on lowering mobile crane-booms, on moving cranes in traffic-lanes away from overhead power-lines, and against moving mobile cranes after dark. This has not stopped an operator killing himself, and injuring someone else, by driving a mobile crane, with the boom up, outside a traffic-lane, after dark.

So there is a real role for preserving life and limb for those who are prepared to look after the safety on the shop-floor. It is by constant dedicated care that accidents are prevented and lives preserved.

Hope for the future

The humanist believes that death is the end. If there is no hope in this life, there is no hope at all. It is a hard belief for the millions for whom this life holds little hope, but it is logical for those who do not believe in God. It leads the humanist to make tremendous efforts on behalf of those who are still alive – and thus from a humanist standpoint have hope – whatever evil things they may have done in the past. They are anxious that murderers who say that they have repented should be paroled and given another chance with the only life they have. But against this view it is argued that society still needs protection and it cannot possibly know for certain whether or not a person has repented.

The Christian believes that repentance is towards God. Even a murderer can be forgiven by God. But in this life none of us is free from sin. 'If we say we have no sin we deceive ourselves.' So of course a child murderer can repent. God can forgive such a person, but that does not necessarily make them immediately fit for society. I have met a prison chaplain who received the new Christian confession of a group of prisoners under sentence of death, for murdering warders in a prison riot. They accepted their sentences as just, and died ready to meet God.

But it is also possible that those who have done wrong feel remorse, and wish they had not committed the deed. Remorse is not the same as repentance. Repentance is not merely turning over a new leaf, a new year's resolution that we will stay off the bottle, be kinder to the family, stop fiddling the tax, drive more carefully. Repentance means acknowledging that we are sinners. We have no power to save ourselves. We have disobeyed the God who made us, who gave us life, health, family, food, shelter, clothing. We have ignored him. He is entitled, and indeed, because he is holy and just, he is obliged to punish us. King David said to God, 'Against you and you only have I sinned.'

The Christian believes that Christ came to earth to save us from that punishment. He stood in our place, suffering death and, in that death, banishment from God, so that those who trust in his death should not perish but have eternal life.

The Christian believes that death is not the end. As all our instincts tell us, man was made to live, and not to die. Death takes us out of a sinful world and a sinful body. Man's instinct is that he was made for better things, as he is. But as Christ said, 'I am the way, the truth and the life. No man comes to the father but by me.'

Chapter 7
Marriage matters

You shall not commit adultery.

There is no command to which our own generation is so opposed as the seventh, which prohibits adultery. Young people take promiscuity for granted. An increasing number of their elders are divorced and remarried. Even in the Christian churches, objections to divorce are diminishing. How can this command remain valid against the tide of opinion? What has changed public opinion?

Doubtless one of the major factors is the widespread availability of fairly safe contraception, especially the contraceptive pill. Most people recognize that children need a stable family. Most women who bear children want a husband with whom to share the responsibility. For these reasons there has been strong resistance throughout the ages to sexual relations outside wedlock. Women have said 'no' whatever their feelings. Men who tried to persuade them against their judgement were suspect. The birth of a child was evidence of promiscuity, and a hazard and complication which restrained both men and women.

But today relationships can be treated as casual. Easy come, easy go, no yesterdays and no tomorrows, an affair of the moment, with no commitment on either side. So the Christian position seems old-fashioned, formed to protect women when they needed protection, and now unnecessary with that need gone.

Few people think through a justification for casual relationships and adultery. Everybody does it, and those who do not would like to if they could. So why not? This is the philosophy of existentialism, though most of those who follow it have never heard of the word. We are here today and gone tomorrow. We should make the best of the moments we have, for who can tell what will come afterwards.

Sensuality is not the only philosophy. Romanticism plays a part. To the romantic, 'love' is the key. If a couple are no longer in love, that justifies the separation. Love must not be frustrated. Love must find a way. It must overcome the obstacles put in its way by the traditions and and shibboleths of society. Love must triumph in the end. Such is the theme of ten thousand novels, and thousands of films and plays.

But some people feel the need for a more rational position. So we have the argument that we have now 'come of age' as a society. Having become adult, we have no need for the strict rules which bound us in more primitive times. If people make mistakes in their marriage, they should be allowed to put them right in a civilized way. Jealous wives should not stand in the way, as they did in more primitive societies. Nor should parents fuss about the young, who are much more knowledgeable and sophisticated, and mature earlier. Why should they be tied down to marriage, when they have to take degrees and train in professions? It is more than we can expect to ask them to keep themselves exclusively for the person they eventually marry. It is argued that nobody in our society ought to insist on marrying a virgin as they did in more primitive societies. This is how the sophisticates of the permissive society argue with their stunted consciences.

An exclusive partnership

Before we answer them directly, we ought to look at the Christian position. For there are always those who want to retain the respectability which the Christian faith still gives, but also to accommodate to secular opinion. So we always have to make sure what Christ and the apostles actually taught.

When Christ was asked about divorce, he pointed back to the beginning – 'from the beginning it was not so.' At the beginning, God instituted marriage because 'It is not good that the man should be alone'. At the beginning it was also a lifelong and exclusive partnership.

Not until we get to the story of Abraham do we come across any corruption of the ideal. Abraham, anxious to provide a male heir, and not willing to wait for the fulfilment of God's promise, took Hagar, his wife Sarah's handmaid. His decision ended in disaster. The two women could not live in the same house, and Hagar and her son had to go.

Throughout the Old Testament we find stories giving the same sad ending. Jacob's two wives were in constant tension, and his family was unruly, selling one brother, Joseph, into slavery. We read of Hannah, Samuel's mother, whose husband had another wife, that 'her rival used to provoke her sorely, to irritate her'. King David had several wives and an impossibly unruly family. His troubles culminated in the rebellion and death of his son Absalom. Of David's successor we read, 'When Solomon was old, his wives turned away his heart after other gods.' As punishment, God took away all of the kingdom, except Judah, from his line.

Nowhere in the Old Testament do we read of a happy marriage to more than one wife. So we are justified in concluding that it does not work out. It was not meant to be like this. There is no reason why it should work out. It is the practice of polygamy. Today we practise a variation of polygamy, what a Muslim friend of mine calls 'serial polygamy'. 'You can have as many wives as you like so long as you have them one at a time.'

Polygamy needs money. Three cannot live as cheaply as two. Economically the poor man could not do it, whether right or wrong. The alternative in biblical times was to put away his first wife. If she had no family to go back to, she was destitute. So the Law of Moses regularized the position. A man was not allowed to put away his wife without divorce proceedings, and there had to be 'a writing of divorcement'.

This was still contrary to the moral law. It was introduced, as Christ said, 'for the hardness of your hearts'. He taught that divorce was morally wrong, whatever the civil law allowed. In the Sermon on the Mount he said, 'Every one who divorces his wife, except on the ground of unchastity, makes her an adulteress; and whoever marries a divorced woman, commits adultery.' In Mark's Gospel this is spelt out. When a man is united to his wife, 'the two shall become one flesh'. Christ continues, 'what God has joined together, let not man separate.'

So marriage is not a matter of mutual convenience, to be put aside when it becomes inconvenient. It is not solely between the two people themselves, to be terminated should they so decide. God has made the union possible. He has done it for companionship, and so that the partners should be fruitful. It is God who has made marriage an 'honourable' estate. So it is not a casual relationship, hidden from sight. It is a public relationship, before both man and God. The only exception made by Christ is that if one party puts asunder what God has joined, then the innocent party is free.

We find the Christian doctrine of marriage developed in the New Testament letters. Some of the new converts to Christianity had more than one wife. This was not the ideal, but they are not told to put away their later wives. However, nobody with more than one wife was allowed to hold office in the church. The rule of monogamy has come to be accepted among Christians.

Marriage is still popular

Although marriage as an institution has come under severe strain, we have to remember that for most people in most parts of the world, it is still the rule. God who made us, made marriage for us. It is natural, and therefore it takes a lot to destroy it.

In a survey carried out by Marplan on behalf of *The Sun* newspaper in July 1977, seven out of ten married men and women thought marriage a '*very* good way of life'. Less than three in a hundred considered it a poor way of living. Asked whether, as time passed, family life became happier and more rewarding, two out of three married men and women said 'yes'. Most of the others said, 'It stays about the same'.

Why, the pollsters asked, is family life so good? What does it offer? Its major benefit is companionship – 'the feeling of not being alone'. As the Bible put it, 'It is not good that man should be alone.'

Companionship came well ahead in the poll. It was followed by children, financial security and sexual satisfaction, as the main benefits. A butcher's wife said, 'Just having someone with you all the time.' A garage mechanic said, 'Having a lovely home and knowing we've built it all up between us.' A plumber said, 'A good wife, good kids, plenty of laughs, not many cries, a lovely settled feeling.' A draughtsman's wife explained, 'Being able to share the good times and the bad times, and the love and affection.'

Only nine per cent of the married men and six per cent of the married women would prefer living with a man or woman, without being married, but with children. Less than two per cent would prefer living in this way in a commune. The majority welcomed the wider contact with relatives in the family circle. The pollsters concluded, 'There is no huge movement to an isolated life – and the companionship afforded by marriage backed by quite a lot of family contact means that family life for most people is still a happy and rewarding way of life.'

So Christians are not alone in defending the family. Christians may sometimes feel they are up against the whole intellectual establishment, a small minority defending an institution which is inevitably in decline. But this opinion poll shows that marriage still means a lot to the average man and woman. It gives companionship in an impersonal world, 'plenty of laughs' and 'love and affection'. A school caretaker was asked by the pollsters to tell them the best thing about family life. He replied, 'My eldest son looking at me and saying, "Thanks dad".' You can see today's sophisticates saying scornfully, 'How corny can you get.' But the Christian faith is for ordinary people. We read of Christ that 'The common people heard him gladly.'

The insecurity of divorce-at-will

In his day, the Pharisees wanted to pin Christ down on divorce. Similarly today's intellectuals want to rush straight to the problem. What happens if a marriage has irretrievably broken down? Do you force people to live together when love has turned to hate?

But we must look, as Christ did, at what God has ordained from the beginning. We must look at the natural function of the institution. The medical profession starts from the standpoint of the natural healthy body. It cannot diagnose disease without knowing about the body's normal function. So it is the task of the Christian church to show how the family should function; the task of Christian families to show how it can function. No marriage is a private affair of the parties. But the Christian marriage, above all, is on public view. Within the church, the older married couples must set an example to the younger.

All kinds of problems may arise in marriage. The problems of physically and mentally handicapped children, the crippling of one of the partners by disease of body or mind, the care of elderly, and maybe difficult relations. Sometimes these problems will fall more heavily on one partner than the other. But they are always best faced together, each partner helping and encouraging the other. For that, life long partnership is crucial. It is that basic security which today's intellectuals are calling in question.

So as we look at the symptoms of marriages which go wrong, we have to ask 'Are these the symptoms of the marriage or of the insecurity of the marriage?' If they are the symptoms of insecurity, there is no point in trying to meet them by making marriage even more insecure.

It seems to be assumed that all the problems within marriage are inherent in the institution. But the mounting problems may well be caused by a fatal loosening of the marriage bond itself. The major change in the divorce law is the move from the idea of a matrimonial offence against an innocent party to the idea of the breakdown of marriage. The first idea required a complaint from the innocent party, the second requires only that the party wanting the divorce can demonstrate a breakdown. Formerly a wronged partner could, and often did, refuse a divorce, though this became rarer as attitudes moved towards the present law. Now the party wanting to break the marriage can *insist* on it. So marriage can now be broken at will by one of the partners, without giving any particular reason – merely that the marriage has irretrievably broken down. This changes marriage from a secure institution to an insecure institution.

The insecurity created by divorce-at-will puts a strain on marriage which it was not meant to bear. Since the partner who looks after the children is normally the wife, she usually has a much greater stake in the marriage. She is likely to be under much greater pressure to preserve it, and to make whatever concessions its preservation now demands. Divorce-at-will downgrades the wife to the status of a mistress – indeed the law itself is beginning to recognize this by upgrading the mistress to the new and inferior status of a wife.

There are many good marriages where the legal status will make no difference. Regardless of the law, husbands and wives will feel themselves committed to each other for life, and their children will be completely secure. But the change in law reflects and endorses a change in attitude. The number of unstable families will become much wider. The temptation to split is much greater. Neither partner is quite sure how the other will act under temptation. The ever-present possibility promotes distrust and suspicion and this, in turn, fosters discord.

What happens when disaster strikes? When one partner becomes chronically sick, or suffers from severe mental stress and depression? When times are hard and money is short? When children or in-laws become a burden? With a lifelong commitment, these problems are faced together, whatever the difficulty. Each partner draws comfort and courage from the other. Without that commitment, the fear that the difficulties will lead to a split becomes an added burden at the very worst time.

If divorce-at-will downgrades the wife to the status of a mistress, it has an even heavier impact on the children. Children need stability and security, which divorce-at-will removes. Small wonder that, as marriage has become less stable, the rate of juvenile crime has increased dramatically.

Juvenile crime is only the tip of the iceberg. It reflects the extreme actions of disoriented youth. They find the security in the gang which they ought to find in the family. But the disorientation is far greater than the criminal statistics reveal. It reflects fathers and mothers who no longer give to the family the wholehearted commitment it needs.

All of us know children from troubled and broken homes. All of us know from first-hand experience children who do not know where to look for the combination of love, restraint and support that they all need. And they, in turn, will not have the example of a solid family commitment when they themselves have a family.

It is this commitment which the Christian is defending when he insists on marriage for life. It is the enjoyment of a secure marriage which we are trying to defend, the hopeless strain of an insecure marriage which we are trying to avoid. So when we come to temperamental differences, to mutual incompatibility, and the daily problems of the marriage guidance counsellor, we must see them against this background. That must be our vision. Keeping a marriage together is totally different to conciliation and arbitration of other kinds. We are trying to preserve one of the primary natural laws on which the health of society rests, as well as the happiness of individuals.

Preventing the breakdowns

A marriage which has gone wrong may, despite all its incompatibilities, be put right. But it is better still if the young make a compatible marriage in the first place. Over the years, society has put various checks and safeguards in the way of rushed marriages. Now that marriage is no longer seen as a life-long commitment, these checks and safeguards seem less necessary. But for the Christians they are as important as ever – indeed, because of the moral climate, even more important.

The apostle Paul points out that the physical union makes 'one flesh'. Those who are temples of God's Holy Spirit should not be made 'one flesh' with a prostitute. This is the sin of fornication, the casual promiscuity so strongly condemned in the New Testament. Yet this is the sin with which our permissive society tempts our youth, with all the persuasiveness known to man. Marriages do emerge from casual relationships, and a stable marriage may result – but the chances are against it.

Christians are asked why it is not natural for young people to live together. Why should we make such a fuss about a legal ceremony, with all its pomp and formality? This is an informal age; why can we not dispense with the taffeta and lace, speeches and cakes? If we believe that the physical union creates one flesh, then the moral commitment is the same as if there had been a formal marriage.

The Christian church – in common with most societies at most times – believes that this strongest of life's moral commitments should not be taken up casually. It should be preceded by an engagement, and recognized openly by friends and family. It should be recognized formally by the church, for the moral commitment, and by the state for the social commitment. So those entering into the commitments recognize publicly that the commitments exist. This helps to make sure that they are not made rashly, and that both parties look before they leap.

Those who want to break down the traditional barriers should ask themselves why they feel the need to do so. If they are honest, they may admit that they do not wish to face up to the commitment. They talk vaguely about an 'experimental relationship', to see how it works out. But they are not experimenting in marriage. There is no such thing as experimental marriage; you cannot have an experimental commitment for life. A casual relationship is an uncertain relationship. If it fails it proves nothing. So we need less pseudo-scientific language about experiments.

Christ widened the accepted definition of adultery by saying, 'Whoever looks on a woman lustfully has committed adultery with her already in his heart.' So formal faithfulness to our wives is not enough. Modern society makes this command especially hard to keep. President Carter frankly admitted that he had broken it. The trends in dress – and undress – and especially the tidal wave of pornography and near-pornography, make it hard to turn a blind eye. Yet our marriages will be happier if we do. For sex without love is a dead end, and 'the end of sin is death' in this too; death to the natural instinct, death to the natural relationship, death to the natural expression of love to the one we have sworn to love. For all those who are not married, it is best to reserve our best, so that when we do marry we *can* give all the love we will want to give.

Unnatural deviations

It would be happy if we could leave perversions at that. But we now find advocates of every kind of perversity condemned in the Law of Moses. We even have those calling themselves Christians who, in the name of charity, urge toleration of homosexual practices. We should remind ourselves that this is condemned in the laws of Moses as an 'abomination to God'. It is condemned in the judgement by God of the cities of Sodom and Gomorrah. It is condemned in forthright terms by the apostle Paul. It has been held down the ages to be both wrong and unnatural, and still causes revulsion among ordinary people. Whether it should be legalized or not, it is undoubtedly a sin.

When we want to commit a sin, we often try to blame it on God, on the grounds that he has so made us that we cannot avoid it. So people refer to themselves as homosexuals as if that was an integral part of their character which they could not alter. Of course each of us is prone to different temptations. Those who are tempted to violence might try to get society to accept that they were born violent, so they should not be condemned. But society could hardly accept that. Undoubtedly some are born with hormonal deficiences. As Christ said, 'Some are born eunuchs.' They do not want to marry. But that cannot be accepted as an excuse for giving in to perverted practices.

The worst result is that others, with no hormonal deficiency, can be perverted. Their potential for a natural relationship can be badly damaged. So society's instinct to curb and discourage this unnatural relationship is entirely right. Certainly Christians who have the respect which Christ had for the law and follow apostolic teaching must condemn it unreservedly.

Christians must always show compassion – as Christ did – to those gripped by powerful urges, which drive them to actions forbidden by the commandments. But the compassion must be – as Christ's was – to the person rather than the deed, which still stands condemned. The Christian does not believe that to condone a breach of God's law will help the person in breach.

God's law is the way of nature. Practices which go against nature go against our constitution. They put strain on our emotional balance, and do us a damage. So it is no favour to the person gripped in the perversion to rationalize it, or pretend it is natural when it is not. It may not be easy to disentangle a person from a perverse relationship with their own sex. It may require time, patience and true love. But it is impossible to begin without a clear goal.

Celibacy in the church

The Christian Reformers of the sixteenth century had to face the moral problems of their day. There was widespread immorality of all kinds among the spiritual leaders of society, the priests and monks. The Reformers not only condemned the celibacy which had led them into immorality, but advocated positively that all Christians should be married. Luther himself married with a flourish, announcing that he and Catherine would hang the nappies out on the line as a message to all concerned, that marriage was an honourable estate for Christian leaders.

John Calvin said that marriage was the remedy provided by God against intemperance. 'And let no man tell me (as many in the present day do) that he can do all things, God helping.' God's way of helping, according to Calvin, was marriage. Those who refused this help 'vainly and presumptuously strive to struggle with and surmount their natural feelings.

And if we think this is a low and unromantic view of marriage, no doubt Calvin would reply that marriage for life, with the mutual respect which a Christian husband and wife must show to each other, is a far higher view of marriage than our 'serial polygamy'.

The sixteenth-century Reformers had to deal with a low view of marriage within the church itself. Celibacy was held to be a higher state than marriage. This teaching penetrated sections of the Christian church at an early stage. It came from eastern philosophy, which taught that matter was the source of evil. The more men and women could escape from the body the holier they would be. But this is not a Christian doctrine, and was not accepted by all.

The Greek church always permitted priests to marry. The Russian Orthodox church required priests to be married. But as early as the fourth century the Roman church forbade the marriage of bishops, presbyters and deacons, and has held to this ever since. The Reformers answered that God made man male and female, and founded marriage.

Throughout the Old Testament, marriage is seen as the natural state of man. The earliest men and women were told 'Be fruitful and multiply and replenish the earth.' Without marriage we cannot do this. To be unmarried was regarded in Old Testament times as a calamity. The highest earthly destiny of a woman was not celibacy, but to be mistress of a family and the mother of children.

In the New Testament, marriage is declared to be 'honourable in all': Paul says, 'Let every man have his own wife and let every woman have her own husband.' He tells Timothy, 'I will that the younger women marry.' Christ twice quotes the original law given in Genesis that a man shall leave his father and mother and be united to his wife, and the two will become one flesh. Paul quotes the same passage, comparing the relationship of a husband and wife to that of Christ and the church, the holiest of relations.

It is impossible to believe that marriage should be regarded by the Christian as degrading, or that celibacy, or perpetual virginity, can be a special virtue. Without the family there would be no paternal or maternal affection, no responding loyalty and respect, none of the security and mutual support which the family at its best can give. This is surely God's gift rather than the loneliness of the monastic cell. Even the bachelor bed-sitter has a monasticism of its own.

Women's liberation

The theme of a section of the women's liberation movement is that women can do without men – or at least without husbands. This takes the same low view of marriage as the medieval church. The Christian faith offered a special protection and position to women, which they do not have in most other societies.

As the influence of the Christian faith has declined, so has the regard of men for women. The women's liberation movement is a reaction to this. It is an attempt to avoid being trapped in an institution – the family – where the man can now walk out and leave the woman with the responsibility of caring for the children. The answer of the women's liberation movement is to try to put the woman on exactly the same footing as the man. Men should have no priority in jobs. If men can have extra-marital affairs, women can have them too. The household responsibilities should be equally shared, including the care of babies and growing children.

This is not the Christian answer. But then neither is the chauvinist, domineering, male-oriented society. With declining moral standards, women have a serious problem, which cannot be laughed aside or put down. But it cannot be met, either, by an equal and opposite reaction. It is no good matching male sins with female sins of the same order. The law can help to keep a minority of malingerers in line – but it cannot adjudicate on every family quarrel. So it is worth looking again at the Christian relationship between husband and wife.

Building a happy marriage

As with neighbours, the relationship must be based on love. As with brothers, it must be based on forgiveness. But love in the Bible is not today's sentimentality. It is based on sacrifice. 'Husbands, love your wives, as Christ loved the church and gave himself up for her.' Christ loved the church enough to die for her. This is the kind of self-sacrificing love a husband is expected to have for his wife.

Pornographers have devalued the word love until it means no more than a selfish desire. So if we find we desire somebody else, the new desire has to be satisfied. The old obligation, if it gets in the way, has to be destroyed.

Within marriage there must be the same consideration for each other. 'The husband should give to his wife her conjugal rights, and likewise the wife to her husband. For the wife does not rule over her own body, but the husband does; likewise the husband does not rule over his own body, but the wife does. Do not refuse one another except perhaps by agreement for a season . . . but then come together again.' Paul writes in the letter to the Ephesians, 'Husbands should love their wives as their own bodies. He who loves his wife loves himself. For no man ever hates his own flesh, but nourishes and cherishes it, as Christ does the Church, because we are members of his body.'

It is in that context that Paul says 'Wives, be subject to your husbands, as to the Lord. For the husband is the head of the wife as Christ is the head of the church, his body, and is himself its Saviour. As the church is subject to Christ, so let wives also be subject in everything to their husbands.' This does not give the husband the right to dominate. He may have to make the final decision, but it should always be made with reference to his wife's wishes. He should lean over backwards to meet her wishes, not his.

In any group there has to be a method of making a final decision. Where there are more than two people, it can be a majority. In an unbreakable partnership, one of the partners has to have the casting vote. Otherwise every time there is a difficult decision to be made, there will be an argument on who should have the final say. A wise husband will not use his casting vote in defiance of his wife. He will try to achieve unanimity on all but the rarest occasions. He will also accept responsibility if his decision turns out to be wrong. A wise wife knows how to influence her husband, and then leave the decision to him.

But this Christian view of marriage needs a commitment which is lacking in the world today. The knowledge that we have to live together for the rest of our lives makes us think twice before doing something which our partner might not like. If every disagreement has eventually to be settled within the partnership, then differences are less likely to arise. We will think twice before we impose on each other, be more ready to draw back from an untenable position.

But if we want to build up a case for leaving, if we want to convince ourselves that the situation has become intolerable and the marriage really has broken down, then we are likely to put on the pressure, and make demands which we know will not be acceptable. In the arms-length relationship which this creates, the wife may feel that it is intolerable for her to submit to her husband. But the problem is not the Christian teaching of submission, but the whole view of marriage.

Even with the best will in the world, there are difficult times in any marriage. Within the church, there is always a job for the older men and women to advise the younger. There are times when even a mature marriage goes through difficult times. The most difficult time of all is right at the beginning, when a wife is trying to train a husband out of his bachelor ways. 'I have been out all day too,' said one newly-married to my wife, 'but when he comes home he announces that *he* is tired.' My wife told her that she had to deal with a husband who came back from the first day at work after their honeymoon to a flat where she had received the furniture removers, unpacked and washed all the china, made all the beds, cleaned and dusted until it was shining, and all he could talk about was that *he was tired*.

Husbands must learn to spend time with their wives. Wives must make sure that the children do not take all their attention. All this a father should tell his son and a mother her daughter. With the increase in marriage-breakdown we live in a society where more and more people have insecure or broken marriages. It is only too easy for a husband or wife to slip into a relationship with one of these unhappy people looking for alternative companionship.

So couples who really want to keep their marriage intact have to be more formal and careful in their relationships with others than ordinary friendliness and good nature would dictate. Marriage matters more than friendship. Misunderstandings with friends matter less that misunderstandings with our wife or our husband.

There is something rather fine in a marriage which has survived all the hazards along the way. A couple married thirty or forty years, who have weathered everything together, understand and respect each other. By now, they have complete security in each other's affection, and can still be amused at each other's little quirks and oddities. By contrast, there is nothing more sordid or boring than the couple who, under the guise of light-hearted banter, continue their disagreements in company. It is a good general rule to stand together in company. Never tease each other, even in fun, before other people.

One new and major source of marriage discord is the competing claims of two careers. There is everything to be said for a woman having a career. She may not get married. If she does, she will have an intellectual interest even when she is not doing a job. If she is widowed, she has something to go back to. But there is a conflict between the care of children and a career.

There is a severe conflict if a husband's career and a wife's take them to different places. We met a senior diplomat overseas whose wife had decided that her career required her to stay in London rather than go with him on the posting. It was thousands of miles from London, and they could not possibly see each other more than once a year. Clearly his career or hers had to go – or the marriage. She had abandoned her career for other overseas postings. On the last home posting she had been able to take it up again. She felt that this was the final chance she would have to take her career seriously. If she had another break in her career, she would never get back to a responsible job. On the other hand, this was his own break-through into a senior job. The next job up was that of ambassador. He was too old to change career.

Christian teaching would put the marriage before either career. It would oppose the couple living apart where they did not have to. In some careers, such as in the armed services, it may be necessary for couples to live apart for a time. But even then the Bible says 'When a man is newly married, he shall not go out with the army or be charged with any business; he shall be free at home one year, to be happy with his wife whom he has taken.' We may not be able to take this literally today, but we can certainly act in the same spirit.

The last chapter of the book of Proverbs has a splendid passage on the virtuous woman. She is no crushed and spineless creature. She is full of vigorous activity, leading her household. It is too long to quote in full, but there are passages which must be quoted in passing,

The heart of her husband trusts in her . . . She does him good, and not harm, all the days of her life. She considers a field and buys it; with the fruit of her hands she plants a vineyard. She opens her hand to the poor, and reaches out her hands to the needy. Her husband is known in the gates, when he sits among the elders of the land. She makes linen garments and sells them; she delivers girdles to the merchants. Strength and dignity are her clothing . . . She opens her mouth with wisdom, and the teaching of kindness is on her tongue. She looks well to the ways of her household, and does not eat the bread of idleness. Her children rise up and call her blessed; her husband also, and he praises her.

This passage – and the book of Proverbs – ends, 'Charm is deceitful, and beauty is vain, but a woman who fears the Lord is to be praised. Give her of the fruit of her hands and let her works praise her in the gates.'

There is no doubt that a marriage has to bear a much greater strain if the partners rub against each other temperamentally. The Christian view is that this has to be accepted. But it is obviously better if we can find partners with whom we are compatible in every way. There is only one firm rule in the New Testament: that a Christian should not marry a non-Christian. This is a major incompatability. Yet if one partner in a marriage becomes a Christian and the other does not, the marriage continues. Parents can give children guidance about marriage partners. In New Testament times fathers seem to have given their daughters in marriage – a custom which continues in many parts of the world. But we live in a society which is socially much more open. It is probably better if parents do not bring too much pressure, for reasons given in Chapter 5.

So there is all the more responsibility on those who choose their partners for themselves to take a good deal of care. It is hard for people to find their level while they are still immature. This is one of the strongest reasons against teenage marriage. They are far more likely to come to grief. We really need time to develop and find our level. Some marry happily the first person they go out with. But more people have a number of friendships before they finally settle.

There is a great literature on the subject, and this is not the place to try to summarize it. But the existence of this literature shows that Christians feel the need to take special care. Their marriage has to last, and they must make the best of it. Yet the literature cannot always help the final decision. Take away all the sex and sentimentality and there must still be a very deep feeling of solid commitment to a particular person, a spark of fire which no one else has lit. There must be a companionship which nobody else can give, an identity which both partners feel, as well as real physical attraction. All this is needed on top of the obvious compatibility of background, temperament and belief, age and ability.

What God has joined together

The Christian belief is that two people when married become one flesh. This has a number of consequences.

The first of these is that it is the physical union which creates the bond, not a marriage ceremony. The physical act creates a unity which makes the idea of 'pre-marital sex' a contradiction in terms. If it is not followed by a formal commitment, it is a cruel contradiction. So strong is the doctrine of 'one flesh' that a Christian who goes to a prostitute 'is one with her in body, for it is said "The two will become one flesh".' The apostle Paul points out that our bodies are members of Christ himself. 'Shall I therefore take the members of Christ and make them members of a prostitute? Never! . . . Shun immorality. Every other sin which a man commits is outside the body; but the immoral man sins against his own body. Do you not know that your body is a temple of the Holy Spirit within you, which you have from God? You are not your own; you were bought with a price. So glorify God with your body.'

The marriage ceremony reflects the belief that the couple should take their vows before God and before man. It is a solemn moment. It should be solemnized formally. The parents are giving up a special position. The husband and wife are taking on a position. They must all recognize this openly. Brothers and sisters, friends and relatives are pledging themselves to recognize the new position, and to do all they can to help the marriage. The members of the church in which the marriage ceremony takes place are giving their pledge to help. But it is the physical union which creates the 'one flesh'. It is the 'one flesh' which binds the two together. Through all the ups and downs of marriage they are drawn back – sometimes despite themselves – by the feeling that they are a part of each other.

That is why adultery is such a cruel sin. It is a tearing apart of one limb from another, leaving one of the partners crippled. But it also leaves the maimed partner free. It was the one exception which Christ made to the rule against divorce:

'Every one who divorces his wife, except on the grounds of unchastity, makes her an adultress,' and 'Whoever divorces his wife, except for unchastity, and marries another, commits adultery.' God has joined them together in 'one flesh'. What God has joined, man must not separate. But the adulterer does separate and the person separated is free. Christ had to make the exception himself because the Law of Moses did not need it. Under that law, with the harsh penalties of those days, the punishment for adultery was death. No doubt the alternative to death by law would have been an illegal killing by the relatives. Christ was challenged to resurrect this old penalty, and refused to do so. But this left the problem of the innocent party and Jesus set the innocent party free.

Despite this, there are churches which will not marry the innocent party. The Roman Catholic Church regards marriage as a sacrament, or a rite which conveys the grace of God to men. But this seems to be adding something which Christ and the apostles do not add, and disallowing therefore what they have allowed. It is God who joins together, not the church. If man, by a selfish act, breaks what God has joined, then it is broken. The person who suffers the breach is free. The church should not impose on an innocent party a burden which Christ does not impose.

There are, on the other hand, churches who regard desertion as a legitimate ground of divorce. They take this from Paul's advice to Christians who have unbelieving husbands or wives. He says, 'If the unbelieving partner desires to separate, let it be so; in such a case the brother or sister is not bound.' They claim that 'bound' means 'bound by the marriage compact'. But in the context it seems much more likely that it means bound by the obligation set out earlier in the chapter to fulfil their marital duty to each other. This interpretation is compatible with Christ's making only one exception. The other interpretation not only contradicts Christ's teaching but puts the church near to the present position of divorce-by-consent when the law demands only evidence of irretrievable breakdown of the marriage. It may be that in our present moral climate desertion is quickly followed by adultery. But it is adultery and not desertion which is the ground of divorce.

It is good that it is so. I can think of one most respectable old lady, later a pillar of her church, and mother of a large family, who married in her teens. Being fiercely independent, she walked out on her husband more than once before she finally settled down. These things can happen in the best-regulated circles. But they can very often be put right if there is no other attachment.

Adultery is a cruel breach of the strongest relationship known to mankind. Yet it does not oblige the injured party to regard the relationship as finally ended. Many a wife has won back a husband, lost temporarily to another woman. Many a man has been glad to come back. An old general with a roving eye and a formidable wife once told me, 'Never forget number one, my boy; never forget number one.'

The marriage may never be the same again. But we are bound to respect a couple for keeping it going. So those of us who have to advise an injured party ought not to be too quick in telling them to claim their freedom. Children bind a marriage together. So do mutual friends and a thousand shared experiences. The longer the life that has been shared, the harder it is to recognize a breach as fatal. I can never forget the unhappiness of couples I see in small hotels, obviously living out of wedlock, finding it a terrible strain. They are all the time trying to convince each other that they have done the right thing, and yet never escape the shadow of the partners they have left behind, who keep coming through the conversation as a recurring refrain.

· We should do all we can to keep together the marriages of our friends. The best way to do this is to keep our own marriages models of mutual love, trust and forbearance.

Chapter 8
Daylight robbery

You shall not steal.

I wonder whether any of us can have a completely clear conscience over the eighth commandment. Of course most of us are not guilty of breaking and entering. But such is the sophistication of modern society that it is possible to defraud without doing anything very dramatic.

The number of ordinary crimes committed has, of course, risen drastically. This shows the breakdown in social morality. The criminal statistics are the visible symptom, recorded officially, of the permissive society. Everybody does what is right in his own eyes.

Everybody does it
The number of criminals is rising. But so too is the number of crimes committed by people who would not dream of leading a life of crime. But they are prepared to engage in petty crime either because it is unlikely that they will be found out, or because everybody is doing it. Even if they are found out, nothing would happen to them.

Almost all businesses are afflicted with petty crime. The fare-dodgers rob the transport system. The shop-lifters rob the supermarkets. But businesses are more commonly robbed by their own employees than by anybody else. Tools walk off; so do the goods in the storeroom, and the cutlery and crockery in the restaurant.

The victim is the large impersonal company. Those who rob it have the happy feeling that it does no harm. They do not see the additions to the selling price which have to be made to cover the losses — now three per cent in most supermarkets. Since they are spread over all the customers, nobody notices.

But, over a period, all the customers have to pay more than they need for their goods. In total, it amounts to a tidy sum.

There is also the almost-universal fiddling of expenses. Some shops and restaurants are happy to oblige customers by giving them receipts for more than the bill, so that the expense-account is inflated. Other employees simply use the time-honoured device of rounding up all their costs. Expenses are tax-free, so the temptation to make a bit on the side can be considerable. Yet nobody is ever going to make his fortune on petty pilferage. The risks of being found out can prevent those who have their record blotted from getting a job of real trust. It is odd that otherwise sensible people will risk their reputation for so little. A talk to somebody just out of prison, his reputation shattered, all his good works discounted, no re-sponsible job open to him, would warn us. One would have thought that even conscience would have been worth more to a man than that. A clear conscience is surely worth more than a few pounds a week.

The cash sub-culture

When we come to tax evasion, we begin to get into the bigger figures. Foolishly we tax what people contribute to the economy, rather than what they take out of it. This puts people into the position where, if they work officially for somebody, they are taxed at thirty per cent or more. But if they work un-officially, they are paid in cash, and the tax collector is none the wiser. The temptations are considerable, especially as the tax rates rise to sixty per cent. So increasingly people have moved into what is known as the 'cash sub-culture'. All odd-jobs are paid in cash. Companies are tempted to pay overtime in cash, and describe it as something else. If they do not, their employees start moonlighting, taking second jobs in the cash sub-culture, rather than working overtime at their official job.

Tax evasion is illegal. Tax avoidance is not. Tax avoidance is the process of so arranging your income as not to attract the maximum liability for tax. But as the Scottish judge, Lord Clyde, said 'No man in this country is under the smallest obligation, legal or other, so to arrange his legal relations to his business or his property so as to enable the Inland Revenue to put the largest possible shovel into his stores.' In the House of Lords, Lord Sumner said, 'The subject is entitled to arrange his affairs so as not to attract taxes imposed by the crown, so far as he can do so within the law.'

There is no principle of 'equity' in tax law. If you are within the letter, however unfairly, you are caught; if you are outside, however unfairly, you escape taxation. On the other hand, the elaborate schemes of the tax-avoidance industry have been condemned by a former Lord Chancellor, Lord Simon, who said 'There is no doubt they are within their legal rights, but that is no reason why their efforts should be regarded as a commendable exercise in ingenuity or as a discharge of the duties of good citizenship. On the contrary, the result of such methods is to increase the load of tax on the shoulders of the great body of good citizens who do not desire or do not know how to adopt these manoeuvres.' The Christian has to ask himself how he would feel if his legal tax avoidance came out in public. Is it something he really could defend, or would he feel ashamed of it?

You may think that the subject of tax-dodging is not one with which the Christian should concern himself unduly. But the New Testament does concern itself with this temptation. Our Lord was asked whether the Jews should pay taxes to Caesar. The taxes were quite as unpopular as today. Further, they were paid to a foreign ruler, who was in the country uninvited. But Christ pointed out that the common currency had Caesar's head – he was the acknowledged ruler – and he told them, 'Render therefore to Caesar the things that are Caesar's, and to God the things that are God's.'

The reverse of the coin had the inscription *'Pontif Maxim'*, high priest. So Caesar was not only an alien ruler, he was claiming something due to God. Christ said that we must give to God what was his due. Caesar was still entitled to his taxes. Paul gave the Roman Christians the same instructions: 'For the same reason you also pay taxes, for the authorities are ministers of God, attending to this very thing. Pay all of them their dues, taxes to whom taxes are due, revenue to whom revenue is due, respect to whom respect is due, honour to whom honour is due.'

There are all kinds of ways in which people can be deprived of their money. Perhaps the least acceptable are those, such as tax avoidance, which are on the borderline of the law. In any stock-market boom there will always be those who ride to wealth on the greed and gullibility of other man.

When I was an articled clerk to the great accounting firm of Price Waterhouse & Co., we were told by our seniors stories of the great boom of the 1920s, and the great crash of 1929. We were dedicated to see that company accounts presented a 'true and fair view', and that shareholders could not be led astray again. Yet the boom and bust of the early 1970s was almost as bad. Paper empires were built up, and shares were sold to the public at greatly inflated prices. With the slump they all crashed, and the money which had been invested vanished. The techniques were the same as those used in the 1930s and in other booms right back to the South Sea Bubble in the early-eighteenth century. Sarah, first Duchess of Marlborough, sold her stock at the height of that boom, because she said the whole thing was 'ridiculous'. It is still ridiculous; though it is amazing what our greed will make us believe.

A fair day's work
Perhaps the most common form of robbery today is the robbery of the employer's time. It seems hard at times, especially perhaps with young Christians doing routine and boring work to persuade them that if they are being paid by the hour, then they owe it to their employers to work for the hours for which they are paid. Christians, as well as everybody else, are inclined to turn up late with feeble excuses or none at all, and to take prolonged lunch-breaks or tea-breaks. It may well be true that everybody does it. It may be true that the employer himself does it. But the contract of employment is for a fixed time. We should fulfil our side of the contract. If by doing this we stand out then that is a part of our witness as Christians to the truth in which we believe.

We can also rob an employer of effort. Paul tells the Ephesian Christians, 'Be obedient to those who are your earthly masters, with fear and trembling, in singleness of heart, as to Christ; not in the way of eye-service, as men-pleasers, but as servants of Christ, doing the will of God from the heart, rendering service with a good will as to the Lord and not to men, knowing that whatever good any one does, he will receive the same again from the Lord.' Paul says almost the same thing to the Colossians: 'Work heartily, as serving the Lord and not men, knowing that from the Lord you will receive the inheritance as your reward.'

We have an excellent example in the Old Testament in

Joseph. He was sold as a slave to Potiphar, but he did not despair. He worked as hard as he knew how, and Potiphar 'left all that he had in Joseph's charge; and having him he had no concern for anything.' When Joseph, falsely accused, found himself in prison it did not change his habit of diligence. Soon 'the keeper of the prison committed to Joseph's care all the prisoners who were in the prison; and whatever was done there, he was the doer of it; the keeper of the prison paid no heed to anything that was in Jospeh's care, because the Lord was with him; and whatever he did, the Lord made it prosper.'

Eventually Joseph went on to look after the whole land of Egypt. But he was not to know that while he was slave. But even as a slave, he did what he thought right. We as Christians are also to do what is right, with the energy which God has given us. As the Preacher tells us in the Book of Ecclesiastes: 'Whatever your hand finds to do, do it with your might.'

Christ put it more precisely. In the parable of the talents and the parable of the pounds he tells us that we are all given talents, which we have a duty to use. The man with five talents was commended for producing another five. The man with two for producing another two. But the man with one, who buried it, was condemned. The Lord ordered, 'throw that worthless servant outside, into the darkness, where there will be weeping and grinding of teeth.' Our lives are not our own and our talents are not our own; we must not only use them, we must develop them to the full. We have no right to vegetate, to drift through life. We are robbing God of the potential he has put in us to serve him and to serve our neighbour. If we give ourselves, we will not only enrich others, we ourselves will be enriched. But if we, in our poverty of spirit, refuse to give ourselves, what little we have will be taken away from us. There is no life so rich as a life of service.

This doctrine has become famous in the last four hundred years as 'the Protestant ethic'. Sociologists are now aware that this ethic of work and self-improvement is disappearing. Governments do not know how to replace it. People demand shorter and shorter working hours, and more and more money. The two demands do not add up.

At the same time, we are discontented with a life of leisure. We do not know what to do with it. Nobody really likes to be unemployed. We feel that we were made to do something, that life was meant to have some significance. Made as we are in the image of God the Creator, we have a creative instinct in us, bursting to get out. We know that there is nothing more satisfying than a really creative job. Nothing gives a greater sense of achievement than bringing our skills to a fine pitch. If we are responsible for the work of others, we should do what we can to see that the work is satisfying. We should never treat human beings, with all their potential, as if they were no more than parts of the machinery.

Shop-floor power

We must now consider the rise of the trades unions and their campaigns for shorter hours. Can a Christian belong to a trades union? Are we entitled to withhold our labour? Is union power used to defraud the community?

We have to remember first that the trades union movement arose out of the Methodist movement. The deacons in the Methodist chapels were the first union convenors. Their power of persuasion was used outside the factory gates.

Nobody who has read the history of the industrial revolution will be surprised. There is no doubt that the worker was oppressed. The bargaining power all lay with the employer. So in a country which was free, where the dignity and freedom of the individual had arisen out of Christian beliefs, where relations between employer and employed were by free contract, it was agreed that workers could bargain collectively. And in a free country, where no man can be forced to work for another, they then gained the right collectively to stop working. This gave them an added bargaining strength against the employer, and enabled them to protect each other from exploitation.

A hundred or more years on, the situation is different. It is not that the bargaining strength has swung entirely the other way. But some workers, using all their natural and legal remedies, now have considerably more bargaining strength than the employer. So the employer is forced to concede what he cannot pay, and attempt to recoup himself by putting up the price to the customer.

This bargaining strength is known as 'shop-floor power'. Not all workers have it. It is exercised to the full by those in charge of a vital production process. They can cause disproportionate expenses to the employer or to the public if they withhold their labour. It is not a power possessed by shop assistants, by agricultural labourers, by school-teachers, by clerical workers, or by most professional workers. The firemen found that they did not have it, as did the postmen. It really requires the ability to stop a production-line directly or indirectly, for instance by cutting off the power.

The selfish use of shop-floor power amounts to the old-fashioned sin of usury. It is the exploitation of economic power for personal gain. In ancient Israel, the usurer was the man who would not lend his neighbour the money for seed-corn except at a rate of interest which forced him to sell up a part of his farm. The modern usurer is the worker who uses his industrial muscle to get more out of the community than he deserves.

As with every other sin, there is a vast cover-up – to try to persuade people that it is not happening. The reality is that those with industrial muscle are depriving those without industrial muscle. So a myth has to be manufactured to cover this up. The myth is that it is all part of a class-struggle between workers and bosses, and that the working class must maintain their solidarity. The myth is that the poor are robbing the rich. The reality is that the strong are robbing the weak. The myth is that this is all part of socialism. The reality is that it is the same brute power of exploitation as naked capitalism. The myth is that it brings wealth. The reality is that the unrestrained exercise of shop-floor power brings poverty and unemployment.

The apostle Paul tells us that wages should be right and fair, or as the old King James Version has it 'just and equal'. So wages should be set by moral values, and not by the exercise of power in the market-place. The trades unions have interpreted 'just' as 'the rate for the job', and equal as 'parity'. The rate should be fixed by the skill and other qualities required for the job. Those doing the same job should get the same rate. These basic trades unions principles seem to be a fair reflection of Paul's principles.

Has the trades union movement gone wrong? If so, it is not alone. When the whole of society throws moral values out of the window, institutions which have been built up on moral values are in difficulty. There is nothing wrong in principle with a trades union. There is nothing wrong in principle with stopping work during negotiation. The right to do so is implicit in the contract between employer and employee.

But we have to be sure that we are not bringing undue pressure for our own gain; that what we are claiming is reasonable, and not extortion under threats. If we are protecting our fellow-workers, we should maintain union solidarity. If we find ourselves part of a small group exploiting its bargaining strength, then we should use our voice and vote to help those whose bargaining power is weak. If need be, we must follow the voice of conscience, and dissociate ourselves from what we believe to be morally wrong.

The professional classes have especial need to exercise care in withdrawing their labour, for the professional has a duty of care. It is a part of his calling. It seems to me quite wrong for the medical profession, doctors or nurses, to withdraw its labour. How can we dedicate our lives to the care of our patients' health, and ourselves take action which damages their health? There are others on whose work the health and safety of the community depends, such as the police, the armed forces and services such as the fire brigades, on whom the public must depend, and who should not breach this trust.

I doubt too whether those responsible for managing the work of others should go on strike. They, too, are in a position of trust. How can you persuade people to join your employment, and then lock them out to further you own selfish aims? Leadership demands trust, and trust has to be earned. How can you borrow from the bank and then endanger the security of that loan by your own selfish action? How can you persuade customers to give you orders, promising delivery dates and then frustrate those delivery dates for personal purposes?

The primacy of trust

All societies depend on trust. But our industrial democracies depend especially on trust. They are free societies. Citizens are not forced to save or work. They depend on the mutual confidence of all groups in each other. We trust the bank and building society, and they seldom let us down. We trust that the goods that we buy will be safe, that the food will be clean, that our wages will be paid, and that our pension will not disappear. All this depends on a basic honesty in society, a willingness to fulfil contracts, even if they turn out badly. Societies with this discipline and self-restraint are prosperous. Societies without it are impoverished.

In the permissive society, the discipline and restraint are beginning to go. A society on the fiddle cannot expect to prosper. Temptation is deeply deceitful. Not only does it not give what it promises, it gives exactly the opposite. It promises wealth, it brings poverty.

The selfish exercise of shop-floor power has defrauded the pensioner, and those whose bargaining power is weak. But it has also defrauded company owners and shareholders. It has shattered their confidence. Real growth in income can only come through the investment of savings in productive business. But the private investor is putting his money into antiques and second houses. So the investment behind the working man is quite inadequate to maintain employment, let alone to raise real spendable incomes. Business leaders keep calling for government to create confidence single-handed. But government cannot do it without restraint all round.

There are those who think the problem of investment can be solved if government takes over the savings institutions, and uses the money to invest in industry. But the problem cannot be put right by adding to the fraud. It can only take over the savings institutions if it exercises the same degree of trust for those who make the deposits. So there really is no alternative to the restoration of trust. To restore trust, we need to restore the old-fashioned virtue of honesty.

There are signs that people are getting worried. Rising unemployment – with no apparent end in sight – and falling real incomes have made them look for a way out. There is considerable hostility to the exercise of unrestrained economic power. Christians should lend their weight where they work, and in other places where they can influence by example or advice, to the policies of mutual restraint which are needed to rebuild trust. The Christian church is meant to be 'the salt of the earth', to prevent corruption, and 'the light of the world' to show up the difference between right and wrong.

Church money-grabbing

Because so much depends on the church, fraud and robbery within the church is the worst offence of all. It is the sin of simony, so called after Simon the sorcerer who tried to buy the power of the Holy Spirit for money. In the letters of Paul to Timothy and Titus, we read of those in the ministry of the church who are 'lovers of money' 'proud, abusive, disobedient to their parents, ungrateful, unholy, inhuman, implacable, slanderers, profligates, fierce, haters of good, treacherous, reckless, swollen with conceit, lovers of pleasure rather than lovers of God, holding the form of religion but denying the power of it.' Paul advises Timothy, 'Avoid such people.' He adds comfortingly, 'But they will not get very far, for their folly will be plain to all.' Paul tells Titus an elder 'must be blameless; he must not be arrogant or quick-tempered . . . or greedy for gain.' He says 'They profess to know God, but they deny him by their deeds.' They must 'be silenced', for they are teaching 'for the sake of dishonest gain'. We must not only avoid exploiting the church for personal gain, we must support the church and, through the church, those in need.

Once when my wife and I were in Los Angeles, we saw a sponsored television programme raising funds for Christian literature. Each piece of literature has a returnable cut-out for names and addresses. We were not told what was in this cut-out, but it was implied that those who returned it had become Christians. There was a shot of literature being handed out to Chinese in junks in Hong Kong, and then a shot of a print-out listing names. The programme presenter divided the list of the literature by the number of names on the print-out to give the number of souls saved. He then appealed to the viewers to give enough to save a soul, or ten souls, or a hundred souls. Then came the phone number, and the cameras went to the girls manning the phones, where calls were pouring in.

The hustlers were cashing in on the desire of simple Christians to save souls, and on the preference that some Christians have for evangelizing by proxy and at a convenient distance. There was no firm evidence as to what was happening to the money which was given, nothing about the literature itself, nothing from responsible local churches as to its effects, no figures given on overhead expenses.

It is to avoid simony that churches try to persuade their members to give through the church or to recognized societies. They try to avoid giving which is linked to sentimental or high-pressure appeals. The church is badly damaged by people in Christian movements who hit big money and are not account-able for it except to thousands of unsophisticated donors.

Private wealth

There are those who argue that the eighth commandment is a

defence of private property. So, up to a point, it is. It is wrong to rob a man of what belongs to him. But that does not mean that the eighth commandment can be used by the rich and powerful to justify their wealth. The Law of Moses was redistributive. Every fifty years, the land had to go back to its original family ownership. While we are not bound by the precise civil law laid down by Moses for the children of Israel 3,000 years ago, we are bound by the spirit in which it was given. This spirit is echoed in the prophets, 'Woe to those who join house to house and field to field until there is no more room.'

At the other end of the political spectrum, there are those who argue that the Ten Commandments have been overtaken by the New Testament. They claim that the ideal is that all possessions should be held in common, as they were by the early church, where 'All the believers were of one heart and mind. No one claimed that any of his possessions were his own, but they shared everything they had.' But this initial enthusiasm led to trouble in that idealistic community.

First one couple pretended that they had given all they possessed, but kept back part. When Peter rebuked them, he made it clear that they had no obligation to bring anything into the pool, that the whole exercise was voluntary. Then there were arguments that the food was not being fairly shared. The apostles were forced to set up a bureacracy of deacons, to make sure that it was properly allocated. No more is heard of the idea. It must have died out, because we soon find two of the deacons occupied instead in preaching the gospel.

So it seems that the eighth commandment is meant to protect personal property and private savings. But it cannot be used to justify vast accumulations of wealth, which give power over other men and women. The exploitation of the power of wealth is condemned in the letter of James. Wealth has been used to exploit the poor in the past, and no doubt it will be so used again in the future. Christian teaching is that this is wrong, and to be condemned. James warns especially that the church should not allow itself to be bought off by wealth.

Chapter 9

Nothing but the truth

You shall not bear false witness against your neighbour.

Every sin has its cover-up language, and lying is no exception. We no longer call a leading public figure a liar. We say that he has a credibility gap. The fact is that he has told so many lies that nobody any longer believes a word he says.

There are honourable exceptions. At one point during 1967 James Callaghan, then Chancellor of the Exchequer, knew that he would have to devalue the pound within a few days. A back-bench MP, ignorant of this, but worried about speculation, asked him his intention. He expected a firm denial. In a similar position eighteen years before, Sir Stafford Cripps had denied his intention to devalue, and had almost immediately done it. But Callaghan refused to follow this precedent. His honesty cost Britain about £500 million. But he helped to restore much-needed trust between the people and their leaders, which no amount of money can buy.

We talk, too, of 'a communication gap' between business-partners, between parents and children, and even between friends. This usually means that they have been let down once too often, and find it impossible to re-establish trust. When words no longer mean anything, how do you persuade people that this time you really mean it?

We see this simple problem most dramatically and openly when great nations who no longer trust each other want to re-establish relationships. If one side simply said so, the other would simply wonder what they were up to now. The Emperors of Germany and Russia made genuine attempts to stop World War I. But once mobilization had been ordered, the deployment of the armies could not be stopped without giving the other side an advantage. Neither Emperor dared to do this.

Professor Sir Herbert Butterfield once compared the problem of nuclear disarmament with the problem of two criminals locked together in a prison cell. Each has a loaded gun. Both want to see both guns thrown out of the window. But neither trusts the other enough to do it first.

When countries want détente, they can no longer use words. They must, in diplomatic language, 'send signals'. They must take some open, public action from which it is difficult to withdraw. This must only be readable as a gesture of friendship. In private relations with each other, people make similar gestures, because words are no longer trusted. But mistrust can be so great that gestures are not trusted either. The box of chocolates, the bunch of flowers are meaningless gestures, because we no longer believe them any more than we once believed the words.

Nobody loves a liar

Although we live in a permissive society, nobody likes a liar. We pass over adultery, we tolerate fiddling and petty fraud, we positively encourage covetousness. But nobody loves a liar. A lie is a personal insult. The liar is telling us that he does not think we are fit to know the truth. He may know it, but we had better not know it. It is an insult to our intelligence. It assumes that we are incapable of discovering the truth for ourselves. It is an insult to our dignity. It assumes that, if we discover the lie, our reaction does not really matter.

So we make the lie an exception in the permissive society. The intellectuals of our day may allow everything else, regardless of the damage. But they all, with one accord, say that they believe in the search for the truth – and after their lights they probably do.

It is just as well that they do. The ordinary citizen has never been subject to more continuous propaganda from all sides than he is today. Partisan statements stream from the political factions, from interest-groups, from companies and trades unions. Public relations experts are hired to put the best face on everything. Campaigns are organized, pressure groups are formed to influence public opinion, ideologies of both left and right hammer out the party line. So in insisting on the search for truth, the Christian and the intellectual are on the same side.

The searchlight of truth is a powerful weapon against

corruption of all kinds. The effort to cover up the truth by lies and evasions is continuous. Greedy men want to seem generous. Exploiters want to cover the sordid sources of their wealth. Drunks want to seem sober. The manipulators of power want to present themselves as disinterested friends of the people. The irresponsible want to look like solid citizens. The hooligan puts on the face of an innocent lad. To all of these people, freedom of speech is a real restraint. Every time one liar is shown up, a hundred others are made to pause.

The freedom of the press

Freedom of speech can be abused. Newspaper owners can up to a point insist on a party line. The news can be slanted. Comment can be prejudiced. And the more freedom of speech is abused, the less the public believe what they read and hear. So it is vital for those in the media to maintain professional standards, and to refuse to allow themselves to be corrupted by the power their position gives. But although it can be swamped by prejudice, the truth is still there. Readers and listeners get to know whom they can trust and whom they should ignore.

Democracy depends on free reporting. The citizen who has the vote must know what goes on. He must be able to judge the issues, the members of parliament and the government. Free reporting is needed to communicate to the voter. Many people believe that the media should be more deferential to the nation's leaders. They should not press politicians so hard in television interviews, and embarrass them at press conferences. But those who are prepared to tell the truth seldom have much to fear. I once asked a press-man why a particular politician had been hounded, even after he had been forced to resign from office. 'Because he told us lies to begin with.' After that they could not accept his denials. They had to find out for themselves.

Of course there are always reasons for covering up. 'The press will get it wrong' – in which case we should exercise our skill in communication, to see that they get it right. 'The public will not understand why we had to do it' – but the public are remarkably understanding if you do them the courtesy of trying to explain. 'We need time to make a considered statement' – if you were on top of your job you should have thought it through by now.

Those who are in the spotlight of public interest in their doings should always consider how any action would look in public, and how they would explain it. Those who have not been exposed to it have little idea how their actions and attitudes would stand up in the full glare of public scrutiny. The behaviour of the men in full view is a good deal more careful, and that is all to the good.

By contrast the rulers of countries without a free press live in a smug and self-satisfied cocoon. They are insulated from the real needs and feelings of their people, and from the problems which they have to solve. The ruler of one such country once took space in the world's press to express his views. His country was bankrupt, owing money everywhere. It seemed that nobody in his entourage had dared to tell him that his ambitious development programme depended on the world price of one basic commodity which provided most of their foreign currency. So when the price slumped, the development programme went on regardless – until the country's foreign currency reserves and then its credit ran out. None of this was reflected in the press statement, which was turgid, self-congratulatory and complacent. There seemed no doubt that the ruler, insulated from criticism, had come to believe his own propaganda.

In a society with a free press, these issues are all debated. The problems are examined by the best brains in the country. Experience tempers intellect, and intellect sharpens experience. Gradually a consensus emerges. Governments depend on this process. Ministers are reluctant to comment on the sole basis of confidential civil service papers. They want to see how the ideas stand up in wider public debate. So they brief economics and industrial correspondents, who print speculative articles to start the debate. Then, as the case develops in public and among members of parliament, ministers begin to make up their minds. So the freedom of the press to search for the truth and to expose lies is the basis of a free society, in which every citizen can make his contribution without fear.

This freedom can be destroyed by violence and threats of violence. It needs a good deal of bravery for those who are threatened – for instance in Northern Ireland – to continue to speak in public. They have to think not only of themselves, but also of their wives and children. And the men with the guns, responsible to nobody, can put out all kinds of lies, trying to enforce their view by intimidation, cruelty and murder.

Christ was merciless in his exposure of the men of power and influence in his time. He called them hypocrites, saying one thing and doing another. He called them whited tombs, covering up the mouldering decay within. He told his followers not to be deceived by them. And because he exposed their pretensions, they hated him, and finally had him killed.

Truth and justice

The form in which this command is put, that we should not 'bear false witness', reminds us that the rule of law also rests in truth. It is the business of the judge (or the jury, in a trial by jury) to discover the truth. The truth is found by the examination of witnesses. We must not bear false witness, either for ourselves or our friends. Where witnesses are intimidated by gangs, by terrorists, or by powerful financial or political interests, the truth cannot be told. The rule of law cannot be enforced, and wrongs cannot be put right. There is one law for the powerful and another for the weak. The laws that are meant to protect every citizen are useless. Those with the power to intimidate can exploit their position as far as they like.

Whatever the official church may have done down the ages, Christ was on the side of the weak and oppressed. But the Old Testament and the New are full of the injustices of partial judges, who will not listen to the truth. The ninth commandment protects the weak and innocent against those who try to take away their rights.

The rule of law is not only essential for the protection of human rights. It is essential for the protection of the complex industrial society in which we live and which gives the average Briton an income ten times higher than the world's average. British companies export and import one billion pounds worth of goods and services every week. They pay out twenty million wage packets a week. They hold and invest hundreds of billions of pounds of other people's money. All these transactions are legally binding contracts, enforceable in the courts. Without the belief that they could be enforced by an impartial court, the whole commercial and economic system, which gives us this high standard of living, and the welfare system which rests on this prosperity, would collapse.

This is not an exaggerated view. There are plenty of
countries in the world where the rule of law is biased. These
countries find it very hard to attract the investment or the
trade. Business is done there, but by families who have their
own way of collecting their debts, or by foreign businesses
which demand their money first. Alternatively, the whole
commercial system is administered by a rigid bureaucracy,
which cannot cope with the variety of people's needs, or
organize the complex industry needed to meet them.

But 999 transactions in every 1,000 depend not on the law,
but on the trust between one man and another. The offices of a
great city are busy all day in the exchange of promises
involving millions of pounds. Often the promise will be verbal
– with the paperwork catching up later. Business on today's
scale depends absolutely on trust. People believe that customers will pay, that suppliers will deliver, that loans will be
repaid on the due date. Workers believe that wages will be
paid every Friday, that insurance claims will be met in full,
that a lifetime's savings will not disappear, that everything
spent will be properly accounted for.

Officials have to depend on the honesty of colleagues.
Boards have to depend on the honesty of officials. If this
general trust collapsed, the law would be swamped. Business
would become small-scale and suspicious. The nation's
wealth-creating capacity would disappear. It is a real danger
in a permissive society. Society wants permissiveness in the
bedroom, but not in the bank. But moral slippage is not
subject to such fine tuning.

Truthfulness begins at home

Just as honesty builds trust in political relations, in the law
and in business, so it builds trust in personal relations. A free
and open society, in which personal relationships can be made
and developed easily, needs widespread trust. Freedom and
informality can only develop where there is that underlying
framework of trust. Once trust begins to be abused on a wide
scale, personal relationships become more guarded. Personal
encounters become more formal, and relationships more rigid,
as people instinctively safeguard and protect their position.

People rebuild the tight social groupings of those they know
and trust, and are reluctant to move too far outside them.
Introductions, family and social connections, all become

important as a protection against the stranger – the outsider whom no one knows. 'He may be clever, but can we trust him?' So the streams of free intercourse which enrich a society freeze up. The passage from one group to another becomes impossibly difficult.

Jesus was born into a suspicious society. 'Who was his father? A carpenter! What does he know?' 'Where does he come from? Nazareth! Can any good thing come out of Nazareth?' 'Who was his teacher? He didn't have one! – Well why does anybody listen to him?' The Sadducees were suspicious of the Pharisees; both were suspicious of the Herodians. The people were suspicious of their rulers, and the rulers did not trust the people. They feared that Jesus would win their allegiance. In case he had already done so, they arrested him at dead of night.

Because people did not trust each other, no promise could be believed without an oath. But oaths often had a catch in them. They were meant to sound more solemn than they were. But Christ tells us that our word should be binding without an oath. Whatever we promise, somebody else should be entitled to depend on that promise.

If we promise somebody a job, he turns down other offers. If a boy tells a girl he loves her, she may refuse advances from others. She may return his affection, and become dependent on his love. But if it turns out that he did not really mean it, then she is lost and hurt.

If people are careful not to give the signs of love unless they really mean it, then the signs have a value. Now that the signs are scattered regardless to everybody who comes along, they no longer mean anything. Nobody knows where they are. Not knowing and not trusting, relationships which really matter become soured and suspicious. Within marriage, the suspicion continues and has a continuing corrosive effect.

Trust within the family matters most of all. It should be the place of security in an insecure world. If we cannot trust our own family, who can we trust? In the most distrustful societies, the family is the bastion of safety. But at the heart of the family is the relationship between husband and wife. And in our permissive society, that relationship has become insecure. Marriage depends more than ever on trust. A breach of trust will be harder to repair, so strict honesty between husband and wife is all the more important.

Just as we use lies to cover up our misdeeds, so we use all kinds of words to cover up lies. We gossip, we exaggerate, we insinuate. We say nothing when we should tell the truth, we tell the truth, but leave out what is most important. We pass on unconfirmed rumours, we pretend to know more than we do.

Perhaps the worst culprit is our vanity. Gossip about other people is aimed to reduce their reputation and raise our own. Everybody has their faults. It does no good at all to us or anyone else if we spend our time in taking our friends and acquaintances to pieces.

Gossip is the curse of most churches. It seems so harmless. Indeed it can often be done under guise of 'warning' those we talk to 'for their own good', or of 'setting proper Christian standards'. But how much good does gossip do? If the church is to be warned, this should be done by the elders. If somebody has gone wrong, he should be rebuked by the elders. If a complaint is to be made it should be made to the elders before witnesses. Apart from these procedures, we do well to hold our tongues.

The letter of James illustrates the damage that can result: 'The tongue is a little member, and boasts of great things. How great a forest is set ablaze by a small fire! And the tongue is a fire. The tongue is an unrighteous world among our members, staining the whole body, setting on fire the cycle of nature, and set on fire by hell . . . a restless evil, full of deadly poison.'

Even common wisdom tells us to hold our tongue if we want to keep out of trouble. Yet there are those who, in the name of frankness and honesty, say all manner of foolish things. We are told to speak the truth 'in love'. We are to think of the people to whom we speak. The truth is sometimes painful and hard to bear. We need to be gentle. Jesus did not expose the disciples to all of the truth at once.

God does not tell us our futures. He takes us through life one day at a time. We could stand no more. So we should restrain our desire to shock, to attack people with the truth. We should be wise, taking people where they are and as they are. Consider how they will take the news or the views we feel we have to give them.

We must not strip away human dignity in the name of truth. The new brutalism treats human beings like talking animals. It is no nearer the truth than the glamourization which treats them like gods. We are always tempted to go from one extreme to another – to make man much more or much less than he is.

To defend pornography as part of the defence of free speech is to drag the argument for freedom down into the gutter. Pornography is the commercial exploitation of the tenderest instincts of men and women. It makes it too easy for those who want to censor the vital debates to point to the flood of pornography as the eventual and inevitable outcome of an uncensored society. They justify their censorship by pointing to the bookstalls, the cinemas and television of the democracies.

Little white lies

Are we bound to tell the truth, regardless of the consequences? Should the Dutch Christians, who concealed Jews from the Nazis, have told the truth? If we are taken prisoner by a terrorist organization, should we tell all we know? Do we tell a relative that they are dying?

When Pharaoh told the Hebrew midwives to kill all the male children, they disobeyed. The told him that they had not killed the boys 'because the Hebrew women are not like the Egyptian women; for they are vigorous and are delivered before the midwife comes to them. So God dealt well with the midwives.' Samuel concealed from King Saul his anointing of the young David.

It is clear that we are not to treat the ninth commandment legalistically, without the slightest regard for the results. The obligation of the Hebrew midwives was to God. They were right to obey him rather than Pharaoh, right to protect themselves and the babies from Pharaoh. Samuel's duty was to God's command. He was under no obligation to put himself, and the office he held, at risk from a tyrannical king. We have no obligation to those who threaten our duty to God.

When Christ reached Emmaus with the two disciples who had not recognized him he acted as if he were going farther. This is described as 'An innocent feint and full of love, by which Jesus Christ wished to prove the faith of his disciples.' It is held to justify the tactics which doctors can use to cure patients and parents to bring up children. But the obligation to speak the truth is a very solemn one and needs a higher obligation to take its place. If we make too free with the exceptions, we will damage the trust which people put in us.

We cannot justify lies simply on the grounds that we are

protecting the church – as the Jesuits are said to have done. We should not make 'mental reservations' in statements to those who are entitled to rely on our honesty.

I doubt whether a doctor should tell a direct lie about his condition to a dying person. On the other hand, people can recover from apparently fatal illnesses. Doctors do not wish to remove the hope which keeps a patient fighting his illness. So they concentrate on the hope, and say less about the statistical chances of survival. It is hard to say that this is wrong. There are patients who really want to know. There are others who do not want this last slender hope to be snuffed out.

The God of truth

Deceit is the particular instrument of the devil. Christ said, 'There is no truth in him. When he lies, he speaks his native language, for he is a liar and the father of lies.' By contrast 'grace and truth came by Jesus Christ.' The devil is personified by darkness, Christ by light. In the book of Revelation, the devil is characterized as the deceiver of the whole world. At the heart of every temptation is a piece of deceit.

When Eve was tempted, she was told 'You will not die.' This was a lie. She believed it, and died. Every temptation since has had its implanted lie. 'It won't matter.' 'Nobody will know.' 'We'll be better off.' 'There's no risk.' 'Everybody does it.' 'I can stop whenever I want.' 'Nobody will mind.' The truth is that, as James puts it, 'Each person is tempted when he is lured and enticed by his own desire. Then desire when it has conceived gives birth to sin; and sin when it is full-grown brings forth death.'

By contrast, truth is part of God's nature. John refers to Christ as 'full of grace and truth'. Christ himself said, 'I am the way, the truth and the life.' He said the Holy Spirit would lead his followers 'into all truth'. The truth is sacred because it is one of the essential parts of God's character. If God is not true, then the foundations of science are built on sand: the nature of the world he created and sustains may change tomorrow. If God is not true, we have no assurance that evil will not finally defeat good.

It is small wonder that a generation which does not believe in God is uncertain, confused and pessimistic. It is only belief in the God of truth which gives certainty, order – and hope.

Chapter 10

The true value of things

*You shall not covet your neighbour's house; you shall not
covet your neighbour's wife, or his manservant, or his
maidservant, or his ox, or his ass, or anything that is your
neighbour's.*

I once took part in a television programme on the tenth
commandment. The other participants were an official of a
relief agency, a Franciscan friar who had renounced everything, an eloquent lady from an advertising agency, a senior
trades union official and a prosperous-looking businessman of
the 'business is business' variety. It was filmed among the
chandeliers of the Dorchester Hotel, in Park Lane.

The businessman was arguing that a little bit of greed
makes the world go round. If people did not want what they
did not have, the economies of the industrial democracies
would grind to a halt. Unemployment, bad enough now,
would reach catastrophic proportions.

John Boyd, then Secretary of the AUEW, was much more
cautious. He said that he did not urge his members to covet
anything that belonged to someone else. The girl from the
advertising agency said that they were there to let the public
know what was available. So even in this permissive age, the
smear of covetousness is evidently something to be avoided.

The official from the relief agency pointed out that Britain
was a rich country. The average income is ten times that in the
Third World. The friar, a delightful young man, said that of
course he would like to be married to a pretty girl, have a home
of his own and a car. But he tried as hard as he could to put all
this behind him.

None of this really got us very far. None of it recognized that
there is, in all of us, something that gets out of hand. A
temptation to eye greedily what our neighbour has, to feel
aggrieved that we do not have it too, and to do whatever is in
our power to lay our hands on it. To want a wife and a home is

natural. But the obsessive desire to have someone else's wife, the bitterness that our neighbour has a better house or a better car – that is wrong. We do not want the kind of society which encourages that kind of wrong.

Unfortunately, in our materialistic society, we are all too easily tempted to covetousness. The trades unions started out with the very proper aim of working for wages which are, in the words of the apostle Paul, 'just and equal'. To the Christians in the trades union movement, such as John Boyd, and to others of the old hands who are not Christians, as well as to idealists of all ages, this is still the aim. But when I was talking like this to one senior trades union leader who tries to follow these Christian ideals, we agreed that whatever its original ideals, the trades union movement was now a vested interest. Many members were in it simply for what they could get out of it. And these trades unionists embody, in organized form, what too many others feel.

Although it is, of course, true that a large proportion of advertising is factual and informative, it would be naive to believe that it makes no attempt to make people want what they do not have.

But maybe this is not so bad as the continuous advertisements of conspicuous consumption in front of those who are never going to be able to afford it. The fostering of a growing sense of grievance, which can only be assuaged at somebody else's expense.

James tells us, 'What causes wars and fighting among you? Is it not your passions that are at war in your members? You desire and do not have, so you kill. And you covet, and cannot obtain, so you fight and wage war. You do not have because you do not ask. You ask and do not receive because you ask wrongly, to spend it on your passions.'

An age of materialism

If there is a particular sin of our time, it is covetousness. Materialism is the special curse of our age. Men have lied and committed adultery through the ages. They have gone after other gods. But the late twentieth century is an age of materialism as few ages have been before.

Not until now have governments risen and fallen almost entirely according to their success in increasing the production of material goods. In the past governments have been brought down by famine, but not by a drop of one per cent in national production. War and shortages have brought inflation in the past. But not until this century has it been brought on by pure, unadulterated greed. Men have stopped work in protest against intolerable conditions and subsistence wages, in defence of their right to organize, and in protest against slavery. But never before have strikes been threatened for increases of fifty per cent and been called for increases of twenty per cent. In the past, bargaining power was organized to help the weak against the strong. Today the rule is that the lion's share goes to the lions.

Not that all this covetousness has done us any good. In the last twenty-five years the time lost in strikes in Britain has been multiplied by four, while the value of money has divided by four. The number of unemployed has multiplied by six, and the annual increase in national production has halved.

The policies of full employment, devised in the 1930s by Lord Keynes, are now unworkable. The arrangements made at the Bretton Woods Conference in the 1940s, to stabilize international currencies and expand world trade, have now collapsed. Currencies have once more become unstable. The increase in world trade has levelled off, and nobody knows how to get it going again. It is hard enough to prevent a complete collapse, and another international slump.

We should not blame our statesmen. They do their best. But faced with the pressures of human greed, they are impotent. They make speeches pointing out how absurd it all is. One man's wage increase is another man's price increase. In the end nobody will be any better off. We should all be sensible and moderate our demands. But behind the doors of the 'corridors of power', they are powerless. If the coal does not arrive at the power station, if the electrians pull the plugs, if the goods are stopped on the production line, or if the exports cannot sail from the docks, what can the politicians do? In a free society you cannot make men work against their will. Even in a police state, the government cannot make men work harder than they wish. And it certainly cannot make them find a better way to work, or a better product to make.

Nor should we put too much blame on the trades union leaders. They too are hemmed in by the drive for more, by their members' demands, and by the knowledge that nobody now has to ask them for permission to go on strike. A few key men can stop the plant, and consult the union later, if at all.

Nor is it easy in this atmosphere to call a halt. Who is prepared to forego his own claim, when prices are rising fast? Everyone has to keep up. The government alone, using all its authority, can call a halt and hope that everyone obeys. At the bottom of it all is the spirit of covetousness. The insistence that whatever the other man has, we must have it too, that nobody should be allowed to get ahead of us, that as soon as they get ahead, our differential must be restored.

The energy crisis

The businessman is inclined to say that all of these wants of society can be solved by increasing output. After all we have doubled our standard of living over the last twenty-five years. There is no reason why we should not double it again in an even shorter time. I am a businessman, and it is a view I have often put myself. It is the view the oil companies in the USA are putting to President Carter in opposing his energy programme.

But the problem of American energy (a problem which affects all wealthy industrial countries to a lesser extent) is that their enormous cars, their air-conditioning and heating are using up the world's oil resources at a prodigious rate. The oil companies say that the search for new sources of oil should be stepped up. But the President says that consumption should come down. That was not popular. He was forced to revise the aim to hold the increase. The President had to bow to covetousness.

The problem is that the earth's resources are not limitless. They need careful conservation. Christian teaching is that the world was made by God, 'The earth is the Lord's and the fullness thereof.' We are trustees. We hold it in trust for our own and future generations. We must pass it on intact. We should not take out more than we put back. Indeed, it can be argued from the parable of the talents and the parable of the pounds, both told by Christ, that we should add to the wealth we are given. We should leave the world a better place than we found it.

Of course there are short-cuts. The nuclear bomb is a cheap and dangerous short-cut to defence, blasting men, women and children indiscriminately. So nuclear power may be a cheap and dangerous short-cut to solve the energy crisis. If it turns out that this is what it is, are we going to press on regardless because we cannot contemplate any restraint on consumption? Or will we give the politicians the option of safeguarding future generations?

Conservation is coming under attack now that its implications are becoming clearer. I remember walking round a fashionable square in London during an election campaign. In front was a shabby old man looking at the election posters and muttering cynically, 'All very well for them; they've got something to conserve.'

I will never forget three hours spent in a village hall, trying unsuccessfully to persuade a middle-class community that it would help reduce the unemployment in Dunbartonshire if we built an oil-rig on their peninsula. Our bright engineers had spent their time measuring the depths of the Clyde to find the optimum position. They had not thought of measuring the incomes of the inhabitants which turned out to be just as important.

So it is no wonder that conservation is regarded as a middle-class idea. It will ensure that the roads and resorts, the suburbs and the shops do not become too crowded for those who already have enough.

But it is not just the middle classes who have benefited from the growth of the industrial nations. This growth has come, to some extent, from a run-down of the world's natural resources, especially oil. The industrial countries kept down the price they paid for raw materials, but passed on their own rising costs to the developing countries. Suddenly in 1973 one group of developing countries, the oil producers, realized that they had some industrial muscle of their own. The oil price-rise, catastrophic though it was, has only given them back part of what they had lost over twenty-five years. Although this has damaged us, it has ruined the poorer countries of the Third World.

There are, of course, those who think that, for the British, the arrival of our own oil will make it all come right. But our oil revenue, important though it is, is marginal. It is never likely to amount to more than one tenth of our exports of goods and services. Oil is not going to save the country.

People before possessions

Covetousness is the desire to get what we have not earned. It is an obsession with material possessions. It is the opposite of Christ's view: 'Is not life more important than food, and the body more than clothing?' 'Beware of all covetousness; for a man's life does not consist in the abundance of his possessions.' The apostle Paul put it another way, 'But those who desire to be rich fall into temptation, into a snare, into many senseless and hurtful desires that plunge men into ruin and destruction. For the love of money is the root of all evils.'

It is easy to see why our age is materialistic. We have received all the benefits of the Industrial Revolution, the application of the scientific method to natural resources. We have persuaded ourselves that this enormous increase in our riches is our natural right. Science seemed to make God irrelevant in the apparently easy and successful provision of our necessities. A belief in God appears to be a superstition of more primitive communities. So a material view of man and nature has replaced a spiritual view.

We live for what we can get, to increase our possessions, and not to improve our character. Money matters more than people. The vicar of a church in an affluent village developed an unfailing conversation-stopper at dinner parties. He would turn to his neighbour and say in a loud voice 'A hundred thousand pounds!' Without fail all other conversation stopped at once.

Newspapers always headline large sums of money and, whenever they can, label a man by his earnings. Covetousness afflicts rich and poor alike. We all persuade ourselves that our present standard of living is only just enough to scrape by. We could not manage on a penny less. Yet working people in Western Europe and North America are rich compared with those in Africa, Asia and South America, who live on only a tenth of our income. At Christian gatherings when people from different parts of the world meet, there is amazement that the others seem to need so much – or alternatively can live on so little. But at these gatherings money ceases to matter. People are valued on their merits as people, and not on their clothes, cars or houses.

Like all other sins, covetousness needs a cloak of respectability. The desire for a more equal society is often pressed into service. Equality is an ideal with which any Christian must sympathize. The first instinct of the early Christians was to put all that they owned in a common pool. We are all equal before God. We brought nothing into the world, and we can take nothing out. In the letter of James it says that the rich must have no special position in the Christian church. He warns the rich 'Come now, you who say, "Today or tomorrow we will go into such and such a town and spend a year there and trade and get gain."; whereas you do not know about tomorrow. What is your life? For you are a mist that appears for a little time and then vanishes.'

The basis for differentials

But renunciation is not the same as confiscation. It is one thing for a rich man to sell all he has and give to the poor. It is an entirely different matter when one group in society is oppressed to make another rich. The Sermon on the Mount is a voluntary code for the individual Christian. It is not a charter for confiscatory taxation. Still less is it a charter for the exercise of shop-floor power by the strong, to transfer the nation's revenues to themselves at the expense of the weak and helpless.

In the democracies, there is equality of political power, embodied in the universal franchise – one man, one vote. There is equality before the law and, so far as the law can provide it, equality of opportunity. There is schooling for all, and universities are open to all who achieve a certain standard of secondary education.

But equality of income is almost impossible to achieve in a free society. Citizens make unequal contributions. It is only right that what a man contributes by way of effort should be matched, to some extent, by what he is allowed to take out as spendable income. This is the biblical principle. Wages should be 'just and equal', 'the rate for the job'. The apostle Paul told Timothy that those who served well as elders in the church were worthy of 'double honour'. So the payment of differentials has a sound Christian base.

Christ's parable of the workers in the vineyard is often quoted out of context. All the workers were paid the same, regardless of their starting time. Naturally the early workers grumbled that they got no more that those who came later. The owner replied, 'Don't I have the right to do what I want with my own money; or are you envious because I am generous?' This reply was used to justify capitalism and landlord's rights. But Christ is not teaching the rights of landlords, or about differentials. He was talking of the Kingdom of God, and the imminent arrival of the Gentiles, late-comers in the Kingdom, and whom the Jews would resent. A parable is meant to illustrate a spiritual truth.

There is another illustration of the common-sense Christian view on income. Paul, in pointing out to the Christians at Corinth that he and Barnabas are entitled to their living expenses from the church, quotes from the Old Testament: 'You shall not muzzle an ox when it treads out the grain.' 'It was written for our sake, because the ploughman should plough in hope and the thresher thresh in hope of a share in the crop.' So there must be some reasonable relation between effort and reward, between the creation of wealth and the share in the wealth created.

In some countries, the pursuit of equality, motivated by envy rather than idealism, is in danger of damaging the wealth-creating process. Covetousness and envy create a mean spirit which will not admit that anyone else's work could be more valuable than ours. But the result of this spirit is to tell the best brains in the country that it is not worth their working after Wednesday afternoon, because five-sixths of their income for the rest of the week will be taken in tax. The market-place fixes a more-or-less objective price on a man's contribution. The commercial judgement and the social judgement of his worth should not be too far apart.

But in Britain members of parliament, judges, police and the armed forces have their incomes fixed by the nation, and we have been even meaner to them. A senior civil servant, who came from a working-class family, and had worked his way up to be head of his great department, told me that he has just worked out that he would never again be able to afford a new car. This is a shabby way for any nation to treat those who serve it. This kind of meanness and envy can never do any good. As the writer of Proverbs says 'One man gives freely, yet grows all the richer; another withholds what he should give, and only suffers want.' Governments are faced with the fact that members of the boards of the great state-owned industries are paid less than the staff who work for them. They reply by saying that they need to get the consent of powerful trades unions to income restraint. Otherwise there will be runaway inflation.

Trades union leaders understand perfectly well that the spendable incomes of the skilled and professional groups no longer compensate for the loss of earning during the long training. They say that the restriction of differentials would set off unrealistic demands from their members. 'How can you explain to a man who gets £2 a week more that someone else is entitled to £20 more?' But how do you explain to a boy of sixteen that he should give up the £60 a week his friends are earning, to stay at school for two more years, go to university for three years, and train professionally for another three? Yet the income differential of the industrial democracies such as Britain and America depends on an increasing number of sixteen-year-olds making that choice.

In the end it is not the professional who will be the loser. His skill is saleable anywhere in the world. The real loser, as always, will be the poor. If the skill of the industrial nations declines, if those who look after our savings will not risk them in industry, then employment will decline. A few million more will be out of work. And since redundancy payments are high, and long-service employees are protected, companies will stop recruiting. The brunt will fall on the school leaver. Pensions will fall relative to earnings. The sick and disabled, and all who cannot wield shop-floor power will be much worse off. Industry will be unable to carry the burden of the welfare state.

The Christian is both an idealist and a realist. We believe that man, made in the image of God, has a conscience to which we can appeal. He is able to tell good from bad. The idea that rewards should be just and equal appeals to most people. The idea that the strong should be able to exploit the weak does not. So we must put forward our ideals for justice in the distribution of economic rewards.

We are taught to pray 'Thy kingdom come, thy will be done, on earth as it is in heaven.' So we must believe that if we work and pray for this, God can answer our prayers. On the other hand, we believe that human nature is sinful. Man's heart is hard. We must frame our laws and customs to allow for this limitation. Wages which are just and equal cannot be imposed. We have to fight for moderation, for consent, for agreement, and for institutions which embody and regulate agreement.

A distinctive life-style
There is no doubt that the flaunting of wealth does not help at

all in suppressing covetousness. I was asked by the MP David Ennals at the height of the inflation in 1974/75 to talk to an all-party meeting he had arranged in Norwich City Hall. In the front row sat three or four young trades union leaders. They did not see why their members should suffer while there was so much wealth about. While the landowners could still shoot the pheasants, they did not see why they should restrain their wage claims.

I said that if a particular person's idea of pleasure was to stand in pouring rain in the middle of a field taking pot shots at birds, we should not hold it against them. But I did not think my argument made much impression.

A year or so earlier I was talking to a public meeting organized by Southwark Council in London's declining dock-land. There too there was great bitterness against the great fortunes made in a few years by the take-over tycoons and property developers. There was a strong feeling that the money earned at the expense of the community was being squandered by a few unscrupulous private individuals. It was a time when even a Conservative Prime Minister felt obliged to dissociate himself from 'the unacceptable face of capitalism'. Greed knows no frontiers of class. The rich can be just as greedy as the poor. But when the rich are greedy, it is more notorious and less acceptable.

The Christian church should try to set a life-style which is separate and distinct. If everybody else is trying to keep up with the Joneses, we should not follow. When they go for more expensive houses, bigger cars, more extravagant holidays, more expensive food and drink, we should hold back.

There is no need for the Christian to be frumpish and badly dressed. But there is no need to go in for the modern equivalent of 'the anklets, the headbands and the crescents; the pendants, the bracelets and the scarfs; the headdresses, the armlets, the sashes, the perfume boxes, and the amulets; the signet rings and nose rings; the festal robes, the mantles, the cloaks, and the handbags; the garments of gauze, the linen garments, the turbans and the veils' spoken against by the prophet Isaiah. By contrast Peter wrote, 'Let not yours be the outward adorning with braiding of hair, decoration of gold, and wearing of fine clothing, but let it be the hidden person of the heart with the imperishable jewel of a gentle and quiet spirit, which in God's sight is very precious.'

The follower of a master whose first miracle was to turn water into wine cannot insist that other Christians are teetotal. But he may well decide to stay off alcohol himself. In an age when business life and social life swims in a rising tide of alcohol, it is as good a gesture as any. The higher the social-circle, the more easily this eccentricity is tolerated.

I once found my place at a lunch given by the Foreign Secretary by the jug of orange-squash waiting in my place. It is the more pretentious hosts who raise their eyebrows and make a fuss when you ask for a soft drink. But when so many suffer from alcoholism, it is well worth sticking to the rule. The same goes for tobacco. I am sorry to see, at a time when many who are not Christians have adopted this rule, so many Christians feel that they must assert their liberty by smoking and drinking.

Those who live well within their resources are much more independent. They are not under pressure to hang on to a job just for the money. They do not need to do work which is well-paid but worthless, instead of work which is low-paid but worthwhile. They are not under pressure to take their bargaining strength to the limit, to build up overtime, or to throw their weight around to get promotion. And if there is a fall in spendable income, they can absorb it. So they are not full of anxiety about their debts and financial burdens.

All this is easier to say than to do. Children not only cost money, they expect the same kind of expenditure as their school friends. They want colour television. They want to travel. They think the telephone is free. They like to be smartly dressed. They want to see the same shows, go to the same concerts. They want to be able to put up their friends, to buy guitars and to have transport. They do not always appreciate a simple life-style.

How far can we impose our standards on our families — especially if they do not share our faith? Yet it is surprising how much of the parent's life-style and aims rub off on children — especially parents who gain their children's respect.

How can a husband impose on a wife? While he is sitting in an office, she maybe has to work over an ancient sink surrounded by peeling Formica. Her friend next door has a brand-new kitchen. She has to walk to the shops, while her friend has a car. She is cut off from her mother, while her friend can drive to hers in half-an-hour. She has to dig the allotment while her friend buys frozen meals. She does not live next to an Afro-Asian with a tenth of the income. She lives over the fence from the Joneses.

It is not easy. But there are Christians who take their minds off their material problems. They manage on less, and do not seem to mind. They are too busy to look at all the things in the shops which they cannot afford. They find that if they obey their heavenly Father, he does look after them. 'Look at the birds of the air; they neither sow nor reap nor gather into barns, and yet your heavenly Father feeds them. Are you not of more value than they?' 'I have been young, and now am old; yet I have not seen the righteous forsaken, or his children begging bread.'

On the positive side, a moderate life-style keeps our friendship open to a far wider number of people. The social pyramid narrows dramatically as it rises. The family that moves to an expensive, exclusive estate excludes a great number of people who might have been their friends. The opulent car separates its driver from ordinary people.

It is part of a Christian's duty to be hospitable, to have a home where people feel comfortable to drop in. It does not help to have a house where the furniture seems more important than the people. William Wilberforce, the leader of the campaign for abolition of the slave trade in nineteenth-century England, was an important Member of Parliament. He had a large family and a large house. But in contrast to the stiff formality of the gentry of his day, his house was friendly and informal. He had a constant stream of visitors of all kinds and conditions.

John Pollock says in his biography *Wilberforce*: 'Callers flocked to him at Kensington. A great man like ex-Lord Chancellor Erskine could dismount during his morning ride in the Park to discuss preventing cruelty to animals. After breakfast anyone with a cause or a plea or a problem or an empty pocket might knock at the front door and be placed in his hall or dining room. Mid-morning presented an astonishing mixture of men and women.'

This had been the pattern at his earlier house at Clapham: 'Broomfield seemed a rather eccentric home. The unkempt shrubberies displayed their owner's stray genius . . . Breakfast was the magnet for an extraordinary mixture of guests bidden or not. The table-talk might unravel some knot in the Abolition campaign or a grave moral question, or be "a sort of galvanic stream of vivacity, humour and warm-heartedness" from the host.'

As we go round some grand Regency house stuffed with expensive treasures, let us ask whether we would feel more welcome there – or at a friendly breakfast with William Wilberforce.

Think of family quarrels over money. What matters more, grandmother's sideboard, or our sister's friendship? Money to decorate the house, or a brother's goodwill and affection? People matter more than money. Friendship matters more than furniture. Children matter more than cars. Status depends, not on what we wear, but on what we are.

The slippery slope of greed

How do we come to covet material possessions? We usually start off with good reasons. A skilled driver wants a good car to drive. As he sways round the corners in his old jalopy, as he cranks her up through the gears, peering through the bleary windscreen beyond the dim headlights, he wants a better car.

As the piano-tuner tells the musician for the fifth time that there is nothing more he can do, she longs for a new instrument. When we allow this natural desire to become an obsession, we become bitter – about someone else's car and someone else's piano. We persuade ourselves that we are entitled to such things – and they are not. An ordinary reaction sours and curdles into covetousness. And it does not matter how much money or power we have, how beautiful our wife or how extensive our estates, we can still fall prey to covetousness.

Ahab was King of Israel when it was still a flourishing kingdom. He was happily attached to his wife, even though she was a bad character. But with all that he had, he became obsessed with the idea that he simply must have the vineyard of his neighbour Naboth for a vegetable garden. He offered him a better vineyard – or money. But Naboth said he could not comply because it was a family heritage. So Ahab sulked. He would not eat until his wife had Naboth killed on a false accusation, and told him to take the vineyard.

David, founder of the royal line of Judah, ancestor of the Messiah, full of faith in God, and a wonderful poet, fell into the sin of covetousness. His reign never recovered. He had both wives and concubines, and could have had more. But he saw another man's wife, and he wanted her.

He was not at the head of his armies in the field, but idling on a roof-top, when he saw Bathsheba. Her husband was where David should have been – with the army. David, having failed to get the husband to spend a night with his wife when she found she was with child by David, had put him in the suicide-squad, where he was killed. God said to David 'I anointed you king over Israel, and I delivered you out of the hand of Saul; and I gave you your master's house, and your master's wives . . . and gave you the house of Israel and of Judah; and if this were too little, I would add to you as much more. Why have you despised the word of the Lord, to do what is evil in his sight? You have smitten Uriah the Hittite with the sword, and have taken his wife to be your wife, and have slain him with the sword of the Ammonites. Now therefore the sword shall never depart from your house.'

David repented and was forgiven. But the baby was lost, and his own family rose in rebellion against him. Yet from his marriage with Bathsheba, as if a token of David's forgiveness, came Solomon. He went on to build the temple, brought the kingdom to its peak, and has been renowned for his wisdom ever since.

So a spirit of covetousness can sting the best of men as well as the worst. Perhaps we should pray in the words of the Book of Proverbs: 'Give me neither poverty nor riches; feed me with the food that is needful for me, lest I be full, and deny thee, and say "Who is the Lord?" or lest I be poor, and steal, and profane the name of my God.'

Chapter 11

Christ's view of the law

Nobody likes a moralizer, the person with a long face and no sense of humour, who tells us what to do. In Christ's time, the Pharisees were the moralizers. They were very strict observers of the fourth commandment. They invented the 'sabbath-day's journey'. You could not travel any further. You had to stop wherever you were. They did not like people to pick ears of corn as they walked through a field. This was work – and you were not meant to work on the sabbath. Jesus said 'The sabbath was made for man, not man for the sabbath.'

But the sharpest argument was when Christ healed the sick on the sabbath. To the Pharisees, the strict letter of the law was far more important than the relief of suffering. Jesus, who had just healed a crippled woman, called them hypocrites. 'Does not each of you on the sabbath untie his ox or his ass from the manger, and lead it away to water it? And ought not this woman . . . be loosed from this bond on the sabbath day?'

Avoiding rigid legalism
The whole attitude of the Pharisees was wrong. Their detailed rules mattered far more than the people the law was meant to help and protect. So the rules were rigidly kept regardless of the human suffering involved. If a son had dedicated money to the temple, and then found he needed the money to keep his impoverished parents, 'then you no longer permit him to do anything for his father or mother, thus making void the word of God through your tradition which you hand on. And many such things you do.'

In the parable of the Good Samaritan, Jesus makes the priest and the Levite walk by on the other side of the road.

They avoid the man who had been beaten by thieves and left half-dead. No doubt they did not want to mix with somebody who got involved in vulgar brawls. He was rescued by a Samaritan, with whose people the Jews were not on speaking terms, because they were heretics and immigrants. Christ told the Pharisees that they were hypocrites. 'You are like white-washed tombs, which outwardly appear beautiful but within they are full of dead men's bones and all uncleanness. So you also outwardly appear righteous to men, but within you are full of hypocrisy and iniquity.'

We all know people like this today. They have a selective morality. They are very severe on some things, and have no conscience at all about others. They condemn the sins of the young, but overlook the sins of the old – or vice versa. They condemn oppression in communist states, but not in Southern Africa – or vice versa. They confine their Christianity to outward observance on Sunday, and forget about it in their daily business. They 'condemn the sins they're not inclined to, while praising those that they've a mind to.'

It is the Pharisees of our day who put people against the church. They are far more interested in their position in the church than in the service the church is meant to give to people. Christ told such people what they really cared about: 'You love the best seat in the synagogues and salutations in the market places.' Those who drew up these laws were also condemned. 'You load men with burdens hard to bear, and you yourselves do not touch the burdens with one of your fingers.'

They were far stricter than God himself. We find the apostles fighting the same tendencies in the early church. Paul told Timothy, that these were those 'whose consciences are seared, who forbid marriage and enjoin abstinence from foods which God created to be received with thanksgiving by those who believe and know the truth. For everything created by God is good, and nothing is to be rejected if it is received with thanksgiving; for then it is consecrated by the word of God and prayer.'

So the Christian faith is not legalistic. It is not a list of rules and regulations, which must be obeyed regardless of suffering, family obligation, or natural God-given instincts. God's law is not a burden to be borne. It is there to help man, to protect him from oppression, hardship and misery. We may have to suffer hardship, but there is no intrinsic merit in it.

Church tradition, like the tradition of the Pharisees, can get out of hand. It should always be compared with what Christ himself said. For instance there is not intrinsic virtue in celibacy. We know that the apostle Peter was married, because Christ cured his wife's mother of a fever. Paul argues the case for the apostles' wives going with them on their missionary journeys. Christ told the apostles that some renounced marriage because of the kingdom of heaven. But this is voluntary. It is not a universal rule, and not to be imposed by the church on those who cannot accept it. Paul, advising Timothy, says. 'I would have younger widows marry, bear children, rule their households.' Clearly he felt that to impose celibacy on young women with natural desires could only lead to scandal.

We are not to add other rigid rules which Christ and the apostles do not impose. Some churches have rigid rules against contraception. But Christ's rule is that we should look to the results of our regulations. And if in this case the result is overpopulation and starvation, it is hard to see how such a rigid rule can be justified.

We are told to 'be fruitful and multiply upon the earth'. But God does not lay down the extent of the multiplication. A father and mother with a family of three have multiplied. They do not have to go on and on. And it could be argued that certain countries are already full, and cannot support additions to the population. It may be that young married couples need encouragement today to forfeit the wife's income in order to have children. But even that advice has to take account of the circumstances – age, income, housing – and should not be a rigid rule.

Some churches have established a whole series of elaborate fasts and rituals. These have more in common with the spirit of the Pharisees than the spirit of Christ. Indeed the Pharisees complained that Christ and his disciples did not fast. Christ did not rule out fasting, nor did the apostles. But they were opposed to empty rituals. Christ said that it was what was inside us that mattered, and that external ritual did not make the slightest difference to that.

People associate religion with ritual. But Christianity should be associated with behaviour. There is no point, Christ tells us, in going through formal rituals with an unforgiving spirit. 'Anyone who is angry with his brother will be subject to judgement . . . Therefore if you are offering your gift at the altar and there remember that your brother has something against you, leave your gift there in front of the altar; first go and be reconciled to your brother; then come and offer your gift.'

The outward ritual means no more than the spirit behind it. Without the spirit it is an empty sham. Who respects the religious observance of people who are mean and unforgiving? They go down the street to church dressed in their Sunday best, topped by hard eyes and a harsh expression. Many a character in literature has been based on those who say one thing in church and do another in the house or shop. This is the spirit which Christ condemned.

Christ and the moral law
The people did not like Christ's exposure of their hypocrisy. At first they tried to make him contradict himself. He had condemned their rules and rituals, so they tried to prove that he was opposed to the Law of Moses. He was against divorce, but Moses allowed it. He began by asking them what Moses had said. They said that Moses permitted a man to write a certificate of divorce and send his wife away.

Jesus then explained the difference between the civil law, which takes into account social conditions, and the unchanging moral law. He said 'For your hardness of heart he wrote you this commandment. But from the beginning of creation, "God made them male and female." "For this reason a man shall leave his father and mother and be joined to his wife, and the two shall become one flesh." So they are no longer two but one flesh. What therefore God has joined together, let not man put asunder.'

When Christ was alone again with the disciples, they asked him about it. He was even more explicit, 'Whoever divorces his wife and marries another, commits adultery against her, and if she divorces her husband and marries another, she commits adultery.'

In Matthew's account the disciples are obviously very worried that the moral law is so much tighter than the public law. They said that if this is the situation between a husband and wife, it is better not to marry. But Jesus does not retract. He says that not everyone can accept this teaching, but only those to whom it has been given. So Christian teaching is un-compromising, it does not alter.

Public law, governing a mixed society, has to reflect what society will put up with. But the moral law is unchanging. Notice that Jesus does not simply refer to the seventh commandment, on adultery. He goes back to the beginning, to the nature of things, to the way God made us male and female. Before Moses put it on tablets of stone, there was a divine order.

Then, at the other extreme, Moses had laid down hard penalties for the Israelites in Sinai. In a more settled and civilized society, the harshest of these penalties had clearly fallen into disuse. So the Pharisees tried to see whether Christ would impose the long-forgotten penalty of stoning. They brought to him a woman taken in adultery.

Jesus was being challenged either to resurrect an archaic penalty, or to say that Moses was wrong; to offend the people, or to offend the law. He did neither. What he did was to bring the whole matter back to a moral basis. The woman's accusers were equally guilty, and he challenged them, 'If any one of you is without sin, let him begin stoning her.' They slipped away one by one, until only Jesus was left with the woman. He asked her 'Woman where are they? Has no one condemned you?' She said, 'No one, sir.' 'Then neither do I condemn you,' Jesus declared. 'Go now and leave your life of sin.' How do we reconcile Jesus' saying he did not condemn her with his telling her to leave a life of sin?

The answer is that he was separating the judicial civil punishment from the moral condemnation of adultery. As a Jewish citizen he did not condemn for the breach of the law – her accusers had vanished. The adulterer, who must have been caught too, was not accused with her. The men had let the man go. But adultery was still sin. And she was not to sin any more. So the laws and penalties of men may change, but (as shown in this case) the laws of God do not change.

So in these two examples Christ distinguishes the moral law, which is eternal, from the law of the land. This second law has to take into account the state of the nation. It will be rougher in hard times and more civilized in better times; harsher in war, when the whole society feels threatened and easier in peace. The courts cannot enforce laws which most people are not prepared to keep. In times when moral standards are high, the law can extend its protection. In times when moral standards are weak, the rule of law is more limited. But God's standards do not change. An action may be legal, but still immoral.

A universal standard?

'I don't belong to the Christian church, so the rules of the church don't apply to me.' 'I am a Christian. The law belongs to the Jews. The Christian is saved by faith and is free from the legalism of the Jews.' Which of these views is right? Or do the Ten Commandments apply to neither – or to both?

The apostle Paul told Timothy, 'We know that the law is good if a man uses it properly. We also know that the law is not made for good men, but for lawbreakers and rebels, the ungodly and sinful, the unholy and irreligious; for those who kill their fathers or mothers, for adulterers and perverts, for slave-traders and liars and perjurers – and for whatever else is contrary to the sound doctrine that conforms to the glorious gospel of the blessed God, which he entrusted to me.'

Paul's list covers the majority of the Ten Commandments. The opening phrase, 'lawbreakers and rebels, the ungodly and sinful, the unholy and irreligious' covers man's relations to God, the subject of the first four commandments (sometimes known as the first table of the law). 'Those who kill their fathers or mothers' covers the fifth and sixth, 'adulterers and perverts' the seventh, 'slave-traders' (or 'men-stealers' in the King James Version) the eighth and 'liars and perjurers' the ninth. And if that is not comprehensive enough, he includes, for good measure, 'whatever else is contrary to the sound doctrine'.

From this passage it is as clear as can be that the Ten Commandments most certainly do apply to those who are not Christians. The non-Christian argues that, since he does not belong to the club, he is not bound by the rules. The Christian church answers that it is not an exclusive club; it is more like an envoy representing a sovereign who is powerful but absent and who has given it a warning message to deliver. Christ several times uses the analogy of the absent king warning of his return to deal with those who had disobeyed him.

God made us. We owe all we have to him. And he gave all those he made, not just the church, the maker's instructions to govern our relations with him and with each other. Everyone is bound by those instructions, whether they acknowledge God or not. We may deny that the absent king exists; but our denial does not alter the reality. If there is a God, he is still there whether we believe or not. If there are maker's instructions, they are still valid whether we agree with them or not. And if there is a maker, the instructions are a great deal more likely to be valid than our fleeting experience of life.

Surely we cannot expect those who have never heard of the Ten Commandments to be bound by them? That is an excuse which does not bear much examination. There are few countries in the world where parents have no authority and respect. The really permissive societies are not the Moslem, Buddhist or Hindu countries, but the formerly Christian countries which have relapsed into permissiveness. The Japanese may be catching up with our permissiveness, but they have a long way still to go. The Marxists are positively puritanical.

Paul explains why the Ten Commandments are respected in the world even where they are not kept. He says in Romans that those 'who do not have the law, do by nature things required by the law; they are a law for themselves, even though they do not have the law, since they show that the requirements of the law are written on their hearts, their consciences also bearing witness, and their thoughts now accusing, now even defending them.'

So everyone, however unlikely, has a conscience given by God to distinguish right from wrong. However hardened it may be, the conscience does not cease to function.

No one likes giving unpopular warnings and Christians are no exception, nor were the Jewish prophets before them. Ezekiel had to be told by God, 'Son of man I have made you a watchman for the house of Israel; whenever you hear a word from my mouth, you shall give them warning from me.' He warned not only Israel, but also the Ammonites, Moabites, Edomites, Philistines, the Phoenicians of Tyre and the Egyptians.

An earlier prophet, Jonah, was sent by God to warn Nineveh. He tried, as so many do today, to avoid the obligation. All we remember today of the story of Jonah is the miraculous means God used to bring him back, that he did go to the powerful heathen capital city of the Assyrians, that he did preach to them and they did repent. If God's law can be preached to the Assyrians, it can be preached to anyone. It is the duty of the Christian church to preach wherever it can.

We cannot dodge the issue by issuing warnings about distant sins of other people. The South Africans are the most popular objects of sermons today. The capitalists come in for a fair amount of punishment in trendy churches which capitalists rarely attend, and the unions suffer in other churches. All men, including South Africans, Communists, capitalists and trades unionists are sinners. The question is, what are *our* sins? The prophets, Christ himself and the apostles all dealt with the sins of their immediate audiences. That is why they were highly relevant and mightily unpopular, why many of them were martyred, but why their message also struck home and changed the lives of millions.

Paul said, 'The law is our schoolmaster to bring us to Christ.' Until we see that there is a law, we will not see that there is a crime for which we must be punished or forgiven. Peter could call for repentance on the day of Pentecost because he had first pointed out the sin of his audience and they had asked him what they must do to heal it. When the church preaches the gospel without preaching the law, it gets a shoal of false conversions, people who have signed on as if they were joining a club. Then afterwards, when they find the rules a bit strict, they drift away.

There are, of course, many who will never accept God's offer of forgiveness. Does the law have anything to say to them? Paul's first letter to Timothy shows that the law was meant to restrain evil in what is still God's world. Samuel Bolton, a seventeenth-century Vice-Chancellor of Cambridge University said that the law 'may hold in and bridle sin, though it cannot heal and cure it' and 'if men are not as good as they would be, yet being restrained, they become not so bad as they would be.'

The Christian church has a duty to preach God's law and to set an example by following it. It should be the light of the world, showing the way to Christ, and the salt of the earth, preventing corruption in society. It is against the laws of God Almighty, the maker of heaven and earth, that we will each be judged by our Creator. To quote Paul's letter to the Romans again, 'You have no excuse, you who pass judgement on someone else, for at whatever point you judge the other, you are condemning yourself, because you who pass judgement do the same things.'

Christian conduct and the law

It might seem obvious that Christians, of all people, should keep God's law, yet many argue that the Christian is no longer under law. Some believe that since the Christian is filled with God's Spirit, we should allow ourselves to be guided by God directly. The charisma is enough and there is not only no need for a written code. Law is wholly inappropriate in the new relationship.

Others believe that the old covenant between God and Israel based on the law is quite different to the new covenant based on grace. They argue that the Christian church is not under law, but under grace. Still others believe that since Christ died for our sins, we are entirely free from the law.

The law not only acts as a restraint and makes us realize our need of God. It is also a guide to Christians who may not fear God as a judge but who nonetheless want to follow him as a father. It is not enough to say that we love God. We may love our wives, but this does not guarantee that we always interpret their wishes correctly! Love means nothing if it is not defined.

Does true love last forever? Snoopy, the 'Peanuts' beagle, is typing a story on top of his kennel.

'Our love will last forever.' he said.

'Oh yes, yes, yes!' she cried.

'Forever being a relative term, however,' he said.

She hit him with a ski-pole.

The confessions of the Christian churches all treat the moral law as a continuing obligation on the Christian. This position is based on Christ's teaching and that of the apostles. Christ said in the Sermon on the Mount, 'Do not think that I have come to abolish the law or the prophets; I have not come to abolish them but to fulfil them . . . Anyone who breaks one of the least of these commandments and teaches others to do the same will be called least in the kingdom of heaven, but whoever practices and teaches these commands will be called great in the kingdom of heaven.'

That certainly seems to be clear enough! The apostle John, writing about Christ, is just as clear, 'We may be sure that we know him, if we keep his commandments. He who says "I know him" but disobeys his commandments is a liar, and the truth is not in him; but whoever keeps his word, in him truly love for God is perfected.' James talks of 'the perfect law, the law of liberty'.

It is often this acceptance of the law which distinguishes a genuine Christian church from a cult. The cult may look and sound as if it has a Christian basis, but cults do not like to be tied down too tightly. Under the guise of freedom they can degenerate into licence or petty tyranny, even, in one horrible case in Guyana, into mass suicide. Maybe no one intended it to be that way, but the objective mutually-agreed law is the best way to ensure that it does not degenerate.

Society, too, is entitled to know where any group stands which is teaching the children of the neighbourhood, inviting wives and husbands, boy-friends and girl-friends to their meetings. The Christian church has a well-understood position in society, even in societies which are basically hostile to it. This is because it has its publicly-stated code of conduct against which it can be judged and held responsible. In countries with a strongly established Catholic church, such as Spain or Austria, it is vital for Protestant churches to establish that they are not cults, that they do keep a rule of faith. As Peter writes in his first letter, 'It is God's will that by doing right you should put to silence the ignorance of foolish men.'

What then is the freedom which Christ has promised?

It is certainly not freedom to disobey God. That is the Antinomian heresy, which first appeared in the early church and appears again from time to time. Paul says, 'You were called to freedom, brethren; only do not use your freedom as an opportunity for the flesh, but through love be servants of one another.' Peter adds, 'Live as free men, yet without using your freedom as a pretext for evil; but live as servants of God.'

Positively, Christians are free from the condemnation of the law. Christ has met this charge under the law, he has substituted for those who trust him. They are free too from the domination of evil. In this life the Christian is never completely free from sin. 'If we say we have no sin, we deceive ourselves, and the truth is not in us,' writes the apostle John in his first letter. On the other hand, 'No one who abides in him sins; no one who sins has either seen him or known him,' he continues. Paul puts the same truth slightly differently, 'We know that our old self was crucified with him so that the sinful body might be destroyed, and we might no longer be enslaved to sin.' (Romans 6:6)

And because of that, the Christian is free from eternal death. We all have to die, but the sting of death has gone. Christians believe that as Christ rose from the dead to a new body, so will they.

The standards of the Sermon on the Mount

Christ was certainly against the rules and regulations of the Pharisees. But this was only because they used them to cover up their pride, selfishness and greed. Pride, selfishness and greed were against the law of God, as they always had been. The Sermon on the Mount gives no easy options. Its standards of behaviour are higher than any code men would ever invent for themselves.

We may not be guilty of murder, but murder arises out of anger. We must not pursue our anger, but be reconciled. We may not be guilty of adultery, but adultery arises out of lust. It is better for us to lose our right eye than be guilty of lust. We may have kept our legal commitments narrowly, to the letter, but we should be trusted without legal commitments solely on our Yes and No. We may be no worse than those who harmed us, but Christ tells us 'Love your enemies.' We may be generous, but we should exercise our generosity secretly, and not put our name on the subscription list. So Jesus sets a higher standard all round. He gives no easy options.

The Sermon on the Mount also turns on its head the idea that we have to keep our end up and preserve our rights. We feel we must not allow anyone to push us around, or exploit us. We will be trampled into the dust if we do not give as good as we get. Christ says that the meek (not the aggressive) will inherit the earth. The merciful will be shown mercy. He asks us to live our lives according to God's wisdom, even though it is directly opposed to all the wisdom of the world.

People do not forgive easily. This is hardly surprising, because it is not easy to forgive. A wrong is a wrong, and it rankles. We can pass over all the wrongs done to other people, but it is hard to pass over a wrong somebody does to us. Another driver cuts in, and forces us to brake or swerve. Do we move over, or do we try to show our displeasure? But where does it end? In the freeways of Los Angeles, we are told, the offended driver may pursue and side-swipe the offending driver until they both end up in the ditch.

There is not much future in that kind of wisdom. But there are other wrongs which leave us yet more bitter. The disciples asked Christ how many times they had to forgive their brother – seven times? Christ said 'Until seventy times seven.' The spirit of forgiveness does not run out at a certain point.

Forgiveness puts an end to the quarrel. You cannot easily continue a quarrel with someone who ignores it. A person who makes full amends for any possible wrong on his side, and completely overlooks any wrong on the other side. A soft answer turns away anger. A meek spirit is a healing spirit. An aggressive spirit keeps the wound open, the sore festering. Aggression breeds aggression, and is self-destructive. Meekness breeds conciliation, and so is self-perpetuating.

The message of the Sermon on the Mount is that Christ has not abolished the law. The Sermon on the Mount sharpens up the law. It takes away the legalism of the Pharisees, which put petty regulations in place of love. But it leaves intact the obligation on us all to answer, in the end, to the God who made us, for all we have ever done and said.

Recovering a sense of awe

We are inclined to react by justifying ourselves. We are not all that bad. Indeed, compared with some people we know, we are nearly saints. But comparisons among ourselves are the wrong yardstick – we have to compare ourselves with God's standards. For it is to God that we must answer.

It is amazing how people's attitudes change when faced with someone in real authority. We may justify ourselves to ourselves. But the speech that we made to the mirror, the arguments which sounded fine in the pub among pals, somehow dry up in a real confrontation. Listen to the pathetic justifications in a magistrate's court. The man in the dock really thought that they would impress the magistrate. But as he makes them, he realizes how silly they sound.

I was once on the receiving end of a tirade about the government, at an export dinner where the Prime Minister was the guest-of-honour. I told my friend that he was talking to the wrong person. It was the Prime Minister's government, not mine. I offered to introduce him to the Prime Minister, who was only a few paces away. That shut him up completely. All of a sudden he lost confidence in his arguments. His bounce, aggression and self-confidence vanished and he went off muttering.

I had the same feeling myself once when launched unexpectedly into a dialogue with the formidable Golda Meir, then Prime Minister of Israel. Even in this cynical age there is a certain awe surrounding heads of government. There is an even greater awe which surrounds a royal family. But these are only men and women. They can and do make mistakes. The awe which surrounds them is as nothing compared to the awe which should – and one day will – surround God. Christ was not just the son of Joseph and Mary – the historic Jesus. He was human, but as John says of him 'In the beginning was the Word, and the Word was with God, and the Word was God. He was in the beginning with God; all things were made through him; and without him was not anything made that was made. In him was life . . .'

It is not easy for us to see the greatness of God, or his holiness. But we can see something of it in nature. 'The heavens are telling the glory of God; the firmament proclaims his handiwork.' There is something in a sunset, in range upon range of high mountains, in moonlit water which reflects the glory of the Creator. God says to Job, 'Where were you when I laid the foundation of the earth?' He asks him, 'Did you give wings to the peacocks?' 'Did you give the horse his might?' 'Is it by your wisdom that the hawk soars?' 'Is it at your command that the eagle mounts up?'

Our answer today, as then, must be No. But we argue that God did not do it either. It was all an accident. If we believe that, we will believe anything. It is small wonder we are returning to superstition.

We are warned that the least sight of God's glory is enough to fill us with awe. Peter, James and John caught a brief glimpse of Jesus, not just as the man they knew, but transfigured with divine glory. 'They fell to the ground terrified.'

Our generation has lost its sense of awe. Everything and everybody is trivialized. We have the most effective means of communication the world has ever known. It is their job to make the news, and the people behind the news, into something which the ordinary person can understand. So everything and everybody is simplified.

I believe that they do a good job. But the bringing of great men into the living room through television, and on its terms, takes away not just the trappings, but the very real power and authority which they have. It is one thing to see a friendly Prime Minister on TV. It is quite a different matter to argue with him across the Cabinet table or in the House of Commons. But that is where the real power of a leader is felt.

We have also lost our sense of awe of the law of the land. The whole penal philosophy today is remedial. Sentences are suspended, cut for good behaviour, and mitigated by parole. The mood of the day has been against the authorities, and all that they stand for.

So it is exceptionally difficult for us in this generation to believe that a day will come when, with an overwhelming sense of awe, we face our Creator. We will answer for the life he has given us, and for the respect we have given to his wishes. Christ's messsage is that this day will come, and that we will have to answer.

Today people talk of God's love, but forget his justice. They say that the God of the Old Testament and the Ten Commandments has somehow been overtaken by a God of love, personified by Jesus. But Jesus preached both love and justice, both heaven and hell. He told his followers that he was going to prepare a place for them in his Father's house. But he also warned that if an eye caused them to sin, because of lust, they should 'pluck it out'. It is better for you to enter into the Kingdom of God with one eye, than to have two eyes and be thrown into hell.

It is Jesus who portrays hell most vividly, in the story of the rich man and the beggar called Lazarus. Both died, and the beggar went to Abraham's side, carried by the angels. The rich man also died and was buried. In hell, where he was in torment, he called, 'Father Abraham, have mercy upon me and send Lazarus to dip the end of his finger in water and cool my tongue; for I am in anguish in this flame.' Abraham replied that the respective positions of the two men were just. There was an unbridgeable gap between them.

We cannot appreciate the death of Christ unless we see the need for it. He died to save mankind from a fate worse than death. We are eternal spirits. When we die, we must die reconciled to our Creator, or alienated from him. To be reconciled is to fulfil our purpose as human beings, with all the joy and satisfaction which this brings. To die alienated, but aware, is to live for ever with the horror of guilt, and the hopelessness of the most terrible and irrevocable mistake.

To be reconciled with God is to be reconciled with all God's Kingdom; to love and be loved, to appreciate and to be appreciated. To be alienated finally from God is to be alienated finally from all our fellow men and women, to be in a society from which all love has finally been removed, and where bitterness and hate rule unchecked.

Chapter 12
Back to basics

People talk of Christianity as one faith among many. This only shows they know little of Christianity, and less of other faiths. Other faiths tell us how to save ourselves. Christ's message is that we cannot save ourselves. It was necessary for the God who made us to save us. To do this he had to become a man and die for us. This messsage is unique to the Christian faith.

Other faiths all bear the mark of man's invention. We like to think that we can pile up merit, and claim our place in heaven, by right and not by favour. Other religions tell us how to do this. They have their laws, their rituals, their fasts, their sacrifices, pilgrimages and purgatories.

There are times when Christian churches incorporate some of this into their teaching and practice. But none of it can be found in the message of Christ or the apostles. They tell us, on the contrary, that we can do nothing for ourselves. Rebellion against God is not to be put right on *our* terms. No sacrifice that we can make is sufficient to offset the outrage of rebellion against the Creator, to whom we owe everything we have.

What can put right the outrage of rebellion against the God who made us? Christ's message is that he alone could do it. He said, 'I did not come to judge the world, but to save it.' There would be a day of judgement. But he had come to reconcile God's love for his creation with his justice in punishing rebellion. To transform himself from a judge to a saviour, Jesus came down to live a man's life: 'Who, though he was in the form of God, did not count equality with God a thing to be grasped, but emptied himself, taking the form of a servant, being born in the likeness of men.'

The humanity of Christ

Jesus was truly God, yet also truly man. He was born into a family, with a father, mother, brothers and sisters, with whom he lived for thirty years. He knew bereavement – by the time of his own death he had lost his father. He was tempted, weary, and sad enough to weep. He was betrayed, abandoned and disowned by his closest friends.

As a man, Jesus was not some remote guru on a mountain-top. He cared for his neighbours. He told his disciples, 'I have compassion on the crowd; because they have been with me now three days, and have nothing to eat; and I am unwilling to send them away hungry, lest they faint on the way.' The disciples objected that they did not have enough food. It was Jesus who insisted that they start feeding them – and all were fed.

Although Jesus cared for people's physical needs, providing food and healing sickness, he taught that this was not enough. He said, 'I am the bread of life; he who comes to me shall not hunger, and he who believes in me shall never thirst.' He told the woman at the well in Samaria, 'Everyone who drinks of this water will thirst again, but whoever drinks of the water I shall give him will never thirst; the water that I shall give him will become in him a spring of water welling up to eternal life.'

The death of Christ

The purpose of Christ's death is summed up in what he said to Nicodemus: 'God so loved the world that he gave his only Son, that whoever believes in him shall not perish but have eternal life.'

Christ's death was not an accident. It was voluntary. He went deliberately to Jerusalem, where he knew that the Jewish leaders were plotting to kill him. He was delivered to Pilate, the Roman Governor, as a Jewish nationalist leader. He was accused of inciting the Jews to rebel against Caesar. Pilate acquitted him of this charge. He said 'I find no crime in this man.'

Under pressure, Pilate sent him to Herod, under whose jurisdiction he came, as the Roman-appointed Jewish ruler of Galilee. Herod had no time for those who were stirring up the Jews to rebellion. But he sent him back, and Pilate said to the Jews, 'You brought me this man as one who was perverting the people; and after examining him before you, behold, I did not find this man guilty of any of your charges against him; neither did Herod, for he sent him back to us. Behold, nothing deserving death has been done by him.'

Pilate tried three times, against popular clamour, to release him. Finally he gave in only when the Jews brought political pressure to bear, by threatening to go over his head to Caesar. 'If you release this man, you are not Caesar's friend; every one who makes himself a king sets himself against Caesar.' Jesus had told his disciples not to resist, 'Do you think that I cannot appeal to my Father, and he will at once send me more than twelve legions of angels? But how then should the scriptures be fulfilled, that it must be so?' And he told Pilate, 'You would have no power over me unless it had been given you from above.'

Jesus died because it was necessary for him to come down as God made man to bear God's punishment for our sins. He reconciled God's justice with his love. If there had been any other way for man to come to God, he need not have died. If God could have forgiven our rebellion without punishing it, Jesus need not have died. Nobody who was guilty of rebellion himself could have died for us. For every rebel is guilty for his own offence. The only person who could die was one who had never rebelled, one who was perfect. This excluded every man and woman; so it could only be God himself.

Other men and women have died in a long slow agony. It was not fear of death which caused the agony in the garden of Gethsemane. It was not fear which caused him to sweat great drops of blood, and to ask his Father if there were another way. It was the prospect of doing what no other man could do – bearing the sins of the world. Christ, who was God, who had been in constant communion with God the Father, was, at the moment that he bore our punishment, shut out of his Father's presence. He was left alone – as we would be left alone – with sin. He cried out, 'My God, my God, why have you forsaken me?' But when it was over, he said, 'Father into your hands I commit my spirit,' and died.

His body was put in a sealed tomb under an armed guard of Roman soldiers, who were liable to execution if they failed to keep it safe. It could not have been stolen by the disciples. But it was not there on the third day. The stone was found on one side, and the tomb was empty.

The resurrection of Christ

Paul summarizes the Christian message: 'Christ died for our sins in accordance with the scriptures, he appeared to Peter, then to the twelve. Then he appeared to more than five hundred brethren at one time, most of whom are still alive, though some have fallen asleep. Then he appeared to James, then to all the apostles. Last of all as to one untimely born he appeared also to me.'

The Christian message is that Christ rose from the dead. Since men do not rise from the dead, this was a sign from God, the giver of life, that Jesus Christ was God the Son as he had said. He had therefore, in his death, done what he said he would do. He had taken the punishment of man's rebellion against God on his own shoulders. This punishment was a once-for-all sacrifice. All who trusted him would be free.

Christ's resurrection is also a sign that we are to rise from the dead: Paul goes on: 'If Christ is preached as raised from the dead, how can some of you say that there is no resurrection of the dead? But if there is no resurrection of the dead, then Christ has not been raised; if Christ has not been raised, then our preaching is in vain and your faith is in vain.'

We may think that Christ's resurrection was a hoax. But not only has the disappearance of a heavily-guarded body got to be explained, but so has the unanimous collusion of over five hundred people. Paul, years later, was able to appeal to all of them who were still living. They had been under threat of imprisonment and death, so he knew the strength of their conviction.

Some faiths may be based on a lie. But is hard to believe that a faith to which the concept of truth is central could be based on a lie. It is hard enough to concoct a credible lie. It is harder to get a small number of people to stick to the same story. It is yet more difficult when the ruling establishment, with the most brutal means of cross-examination, is determined to discredit the story. It is impossible if the central belief of all those concerned with the lie is that we should tell the truth on every occasion.

We are naturally sceptical of any story that someone has risen from the dead. But there is in each one of us a feeling of immortality. We were not born to die, but to live. Our personality will not be snuffed out, as though it had never been, but will survive. There is also in us a feeling that one day justice will be done. The tyrants who died in their beds will be brought to account. The great injustices of life will be avenged, as they can never be avenged in this world. If we believe in a God who gives life, we must believe that he is able to raise the dead to life again.

Faith in Christ

The apostles gave evidence of the resurrection of Jesus Christ. Some people believed, and others did not. But they preached with urgency, because the Christian message is not one of salvation for all, but of salvation to those who believe. In writing to the Romans, Paul quotes the prophet Joel, "'Everyone who calls upon the name of the Lord will be saved." But how are men to call upon him in whom they have not believed? And how are they to believe in him of whom they have never heard? And how are they to hear without a preacher?'"

The first Christian sermon was preached by Peter on the day of Pentecost. He told his hearers, 'Repent, and be baptized every one of you in the name of Jesus Christ for the forgiveness of your sins; and you shall receive the gift of the Holy Spirit.' God deals with us as responsible human beings. None of us have kept his commandments. As we read them, and try to measure our conduct by them, we can see that we have not done what we ought to have done. We have done many things which we ought not to have done.

The forgiveness of the rebel cannot begin until the rebellion has been called off. Reconciliation has to be on both sides. God cannot forgive those who do not wish to be forgiven; those who do not believe there is a God against whom to rebel; those who believe in a God, but have invented one of their own ('I cannot believe in a God who . . .'); those who believe they have kept God's law and do not need any forgiveness.

Peter called for repentance. If our examination of the Ten Commandments has done nothing else but show us that we have fallen short of God's standards and need to repent, then it has been worthwhile. If it has merely depressed us, then it has done no good at all. It is not enough to be baptized. We must repent and be baptized. Baptism is a sign of the change, not the change itself. So it is not enough to be a church member, or even to be a member of a Christian family. God has no grandchildren, only children.

In every story of conversion in the Acts of the Apostles,

those who became Christians had previously felt concerned about themselves. Those to whom Peter spoke on the day of Pentecost 'were cut to the heart, and said to Peter and the rest of the apostles, "Brethren, what shall we do?"' An Ethiopian official, the Treasurer of Queen Candace, had travelled all the way to Jerusalem in search of the true God. He was reading the prophet Isaiah on his way home. Philip met him, explained Isaiah's prophecy of Jesus' death and 'told him the good news about Jesus.' The Ethiopian was baptized.

Saul of Tarsus does not seem to have been seeking so long. But by his own account to King Agrippa, he had been 'kicking against the goads'. So although he had been breathing out murderous threats against the Lord's disciples, there was this constant pricking which told him he was wrong. He would not acknowledge it until on the Damascus road there was the flash of light from heaven. He heard a voice say to him, 'Saul, Saul, why do you persecute me?' In his reply, Saul acknowledged him as 'Lord', and when he came, still blinded, to Damascus, he was baptized.

The next individual convert we read of was a Roman. He was a centurion in the Italian Regiment. His concern had led him to pray and give gifts to the poor. God sent to him the apostle Peter who told him and the large gathering of people in his house that Jesus was 'the one whom God appointed as the judge of the living and the dead'. Cornelius and those with him were baptized.

Saul of Tarsus, now known by his Roman name Paul, and commissioned as an apostle, went from Asia to Europe. The next individual convert of whom we read, and the first in Europe, was a woman named Lydia. Lydia was a worshipper of God. She responded to Paul's message, and was baptized, with her household.

Paul, and his companion Silas, soon found themselves wrongly imprisoned. There was an earthquake during the night. The jailer called for lights, rushed in, and fell trembling before Paul and Silas. He brought them out, and asked, 'Men what must I do to be saved?' They replied, 'Believe on the Lord Jesus and you will be saved – you and your house.' Then they spoke the word of the Lord to him and to all the others in his house. The jailer washed their wounds. 'Then immediately he and his family were baptized . . . and the whole family was filled with joy.'

These were very different people – a high government official from Africa, a Jewish Pharisee, a Roman soldier, a Greek merchant woman and a jailer. Yet all had the same nagging concern. All listened to and accepted the same good news. All were baptized as the outward sign that their sins were washed away. All were filled with joy. People become Christians in many different ways. But the same basic pattern, beginning with a concern about our condition, has repeated itself millions of times among all ages, kinds and conditions of people. Let us look finally at one of the most recent, the experience of a young man called Joe.

Christianity is a weak crutch of hypocrisy, contradictions and false promises. This is the perhaps somewhat obvious conclusion I had reached in my early teens as I, brought up on the Christian faith, rejected religion and Christ on the basis of overwhelming contrary evidence. How could evil emerge from 100 per cent good? Why did God let sin enter the world? What right did he have to play around with our souls? Don't tell me I will have to answer to God for my life when I die. Did I ask to be born and have responsibility? Did I have the choice between being perfect and sinning? No, I am told, I suffer because Adam sinned and that's all there is to it. It's God's mess, and he owes me heaven for letting the world he selfishly created out of loneliness go to sin and depravity.

I enjoyed being the non-Christian of the family – the concern and prayers I knew I was receiving swelled my ego, making me the rebel I longed to be. I liked people watching me walk down the road away from the church instead of entering it on a Sunday evening. It made me important.

The trouble was that the lack of Christianity created a gap which needed to be filled. For a short while it was a hardened scepticism, that life was just a deceitful decaying pit where no one had a reason to stay yet no one wanted to leave.

The fear of death was pathetic, yet real, and was a problem affecting me too. A friend of mine introduced me to Buddhism, exciting in its originality. Death just meant your soul floating out of your body and entering somewhere else; if one feared it, one could try it alive by astral projection. That friend of mine did, resulting in an experience that frightened him so much he withdrew from his friends and started socializing with people much younger than himself. Following this I discovered the author of the Buddhist books was a con-man. More lies. Religion always seemed to be lies.

The gap was still there to be filled. Drinking, thieving and breaking the law gave satisfaction, but for a very limited time, and the real needs were still there. Anarchy was the next phase, followed by an almost morbid worship of America. There had to be something more; I needed a reason to live. What was the point of doing anything if it never added up to anything? Even James Dean died. What did life bring him?

I had reached this conclusion while on holiday with my family, staying at a Christian student conference. What had sunk me into a black depression was not only that these people had a permanent inner peace and happiness but also that they felt sorry for me. Me! It was all the wrong way round. It was the Christians who couldn't have free sex, swear, go boozing and generally do what they felt like. I realized I was unhappy and couldn't understand why. It was a question an American girl asked me. We had had one of a series of arguments about Christianity in which I had whipped out all the old arguments, when she stopped talking, sighed and said 'OK, Joe. Christianity is wrong. Fine. Now go away and answer me this question. If Jesus Christ was not the Son of God, who was he?' It was a question I wanted to forget. I knew what everything pointed to and hated it. I just could not rid myself of the faces of the students from the persecuted countries where they were forbidden degrees, jobs, and generally ostracized for their faith. They were happy. The crutch argument began to look weak.

A week later I was staying at a friend's house in Yugoslavia and was still mulling it over. I sat on my bed in the tiny bungalow at the end of the garden where I was staying when I suddenly realized the answer. Jesus Christ had to be the Son of God. Nothing else would fit. Would a madman, spaceman, 'very good person', create a following which disrupted Roman law and order, lead men to burn on crosses, and spread a faith worldwide under persecution? This meant I had to become a Christian. The thought hit me like a punch in the face. Me! Alright then, I thought, despondently. I'll enjoy myself for the next fifteen years and then become a Christian. This didn't really convince me though, and I started thinking about what Christ had done for me and what I had done for him in return. It was then I realized how much badness was in me and asked God to forgive me and let Christ into my life.

And now? Now, naturally, my life is different. I have a reason to live and a code to gear it. My friends, after their initial shock at my conversion, threw the standard questions at me. How could I accept that the contradictions in the Bible were things I just need not know? There is an answer. I know because Christ said so, and he never lied. That perfection is why we know he was the Son of God. It's why he died for us and rose again to prepare a place in heaven for us, even for people like me who were big-headed, sneering and blasphemous. It is why I am a Christian today. Does anyone want to talk about responsibility? The Son of God, who was perfect, came down to save and teach us. He was spat on, hounded, and finally nailed to a cross for his efforts. It happened then and would happen today.

We are all responsible. The acceptance or rejection of God's guidelines for society, and of Christianity itself, is a matter of our own choice. But if we choose to reject them, we must be prepared to face the consequences. If Jesus was not the Son of God, who was he? If what he taught was wrong, if the Law of God in the Ten Commandments is an outworn ethic or an empty sham, what then? As Peter said to Jesus, 'Lord, to whom shall we go? You have the words of eternal life.'